Auditing Organizations Through a Strategic-Systems Lens

The KPMG Business Measurement Process

Timothy B. Bell

Frank O. Marrs

KPMG Peat Marwick LLP

Ira Solomon

Howard Thomas

University of Illinois at Urbana-Champaign

Foreword by William R. Kinney, Jr.

This monograph is not intended to constitute an exhaustive coverage of all of the policies and procedures comprising KPMG's full audit process, and how it comports with generally accepted auditing standards.

Contents

Foreword

by William R. Kinney, Jr.

As the twentieth century comes to a close, information technology has brought dramatic changes to business processes, to business organization, and even to auditing. These changes require major reconsideration of what we know about financial-statement audit technology. This monograph presents the thinking of two leading practitioners and two leading scholars on the foundations of auditing technology for the twenty-first century.

With changes in information technology, the inherent reliability of information systems for routine transactions processing is substantially increased, controls over transactions are increasingly embedded in software, and extensive data on nonfinancial dimensions of business performance are economical for audit use. But because information technology and deregulation have lowered barriers to entry in many industries, a company can lose viability quickly, making financial statements less reliable predictors of the future. Therefore, analysis of business viability is an important determinant of the value of audited financial statements.

This monograph makes it clear that business viability and profitability assessments are essential elements of financial-statement auditing today and for the twenty-first century. The authors also make it clear that the viability of the whole of a business is more than the sum of its parts. The individual financial-statement elements can be valid, yet the entity as a whole not be viable because of the complex interdependencies comprising business viability. The monograph focuses on analyses of strategy, business processes to achieve strategy, key indicators necessary to monitor performance of business processes in achieving strategy, and risks faced by an entity.

"Understanding the client's business" is not a new concept, and neither is the idea of a "top down" approach to financial-statement auditing. References to both can be found in the 1960s in audit manuals of large CPA firms. What is new is a serious attempt to provide guidance to field auditors applying these concepts. Serious thought, formal analysis of an entity's strategy, and whether it can be achieved have not been financial-statement audit steps. KPMG's Business Measurement Process (BMP) approach makes common this type of thoughtful analysis. The viability of a business is formally considered, and it provides a basis for forming expectations about what should be the financial-statement balances for the audit period. If an entity has a viable strategy, reasonable plans, effective internal control, and account balances that are close to expectations, then the need for detailed auditing is limited to exceptional items.

The monograph includes a review of the history of auditing practice, how it is changing, and how BMP satisfies auditing standards. In addition, the authors provide numerous references to concepts outside traditional auditing thought. These references can form a basis for research by scholars and practitioners. Furthermore, the monograph contains numerous phrases beginning with "we believe." Some of the "we believes" are straightforward and not controversial. Others are controversial, and should be subjected to systematic inquiry. To me, this is a major contribution of the monograph — it can lead to thoughtful research by scholars and practitioners.

The monograph also contains implications for what should be the accounting, auditing, and business curriculum for the twenty-first century. Clearly information technology will be important, as will how best to measure key performance factors, including nonfinancial measures. In addition, education for assurance services that considers both the relevance and reliability of information for decision-makers, and the relation of information to strategy and strategy implementation will be essential.

William R. Kinney, Jr.
Charles and Elizabeth Prothro Regents Chair in Business
and
Price Waterhouse Auditing Fellow
Graduate School of Business
University of Texas at Austin

July 14, 1997

Preface

Organizations are now interconnecting to their diverse and rapidly changing environments in ways never before imagined. For example, information about products, prices, inventory on hand, shipping arrangements, customer service, and for product troubleshooting can now be accessed quickly and easily by current and potential customers and suppliers through organizations' web sites. Organizations are beginning to transact business in the paperless "virtual web world" where they can reduce the overhead costs associated with traditional forms of customer interface, e.g., by replacing physical retail stores and sales personnel with virtual on-line stores.

In their quest to provide higher-quality products and services at lower costs, some organizations are shedding noncore processes, choosing instead to interconnect to outside providers who can service the organizations' and customers' needs more efficiently and effectively. Strategic alliances are being formed with increasing frequency to establish new economic niches, e.g., Microsoft and NBC. In many industries, long-lived strategies and related competitive advantages that once served organizations well are no longer viable. Increasingly, managers are recognizing that in today's rapidly changing economy they must continuously scan their environments for external forces that threaten the viability of their current strategies. And, managers are becoming increasingly aware that for an organization to survive, managers not only must be prepared to reorient their strategies on short notice, but the organization must be nimble enough to adapt its technologies and core processes so that the organization can establish a presence in emerging niches before its competitors.

One consequence of the accelerating rate of change in the global economy, and of the expanding number and variety of interdependencies among economic agents, is that it is increasingly important for the financial-statement audit to be conducted with the recognition that the client organization is not a free-standing entity. Just as one cannot remove a single piece from a mosaic and derive meaning from it, one cannot effectively remove the client organization from the broader economic web of which it is a part and expect to gain an accurate understanding of the entity's transactions and its entity-level performance and financial condition. That is, whether one is speaking about a single piece of a mosaic or a set of financial statements, full understanding only can be achieved by a study of the whole "system."

In one sense this theme is not new. Authoritative guidance has for many years recognized that auditors need knowledge of the client organization's operations and industry. What is new, however, is that the level of complexity and myriad interconnections inherent in today's global economy have significant implications for the requisite scope and role of such knowledge in the performance of a financial-statement audit. In this monograph we present our ideas about these and other features of the business knowledge needed to perform the audit in the new millennium, and we illustrate how these ideas can be operationalized by describing one audit approach that embraces them — KPMG Peat Marwick's Business Measurement Process.

We envision three primary audiences for this monograph. First, the monograph is intended to communicate to the academic community the aforementioned ideas. Importantly, however, the academic community we hope to reach extends beyond accounting and auditing to the fields of strategy, systems, and management. Our hope is to engage members of these communities sufficiently so that they will want to work on further developing some of the ideas contained in the monograph. Second, the monograph is intended to communicate to auditing policy-makers and to the business community at large our ideas about how technological and related changes are affecting the audit approach of a Big-6 firm. Here the desire is to stimulate a dialogue and ultimately improve the value of the financial-statement audit on a profession-wide basis. The third audience is students — future practitioners and consumers of auditing services. It is our hope that some of the ideas contained in the monograph will find their way into business school curricula, thereby influencing how students are introduced to financial-statement auditing.

We gratefully acknowledge the valuable feedback provided by the following individuals on earlier versions of this monograph: Clif Brown, John Chandler, Fred Neumann, and Dan Stone from the University of Illinois at Urbana-Champaign; Bill Felix from the University of Arizona; Bill Kinney from the University of Texas at Austin; and Robert Knechel from the University of Florida.

Each of us has found the process of writing this monograph to be an exceptional learning experience. We are excited about additional learning opportunities created as a consequence of the ideas provided by the readers of this monograph.

Timothy B. Bell

Director, Assurance Services
KPMG Peat Marwick LLP

Frank O. Marrs

Partner-in-Charge,
Assurance Services
KPMG Peat Marwick LLP

Ira Solomon

KPMG Peat Marwick Distinguished
Professor of Accountancy
University of Illinois
at Urbana-Champaign

Howard Thomas

Dean, College of Commerce
James F. Towey Professor
of Strategic Management
University of Illinois
at Urbana-Champaign

August 8, 1997

1 Introduction

In our time, the confidence, maturity and promise of a science
should be measured not by its power to reduce the complex to the
simple . . . but instead by its willingness to study complexity with
advanced methods under descriptions that respect the reality of
what is being studied.

David J. Depew and Bruce H. Weber
Evolution, Ethics, and the Complexity Revolution[1]

Accounting plays a central role in the efficient allocation of resources in market-based economies. By adding credibility to accounting measurements and disclosures, auditing has for centuries made it possible for accounting to play such a key role. Today's global economy and the business organizations operating within it, however, have become so complex and interdependent that new approaches to auditing must be developed. With these new approaches, the auditor would embrace and master, rather than simplify, the complexity inherent in the economic web of interrelationships of which the client organization is a part. Such approaches can serve the auditor's primary assurance goal by providing a greater power to detect material misstatements while concurrently creating auditing efficiencies.

The authoritative pronouncements on auditing make numerous references to the need to understand the client's business and industry when performing a financial-statement audit. Knowledge about the nature of the client's business activities and related business risks, its organizational structure and internal environment, and its relationships and interactions with its external environment, provides a basis for the auditor's evaluation of whether financial-statement assertions are valid. In today's complex and dynamic economic world, obtaining this knowledge is a formidable undertaking. It entails identifying, collecting, and processing a wealth of information about the client's business and industry that may be relevant to the audit. And, more importantly, it entails integrating this information to form a "whole-system" representation of how the client organization fits within the broader economic environment, and how effectively its key business processes, working in combination, maintain or strengthen that fit.

1 David J. Depew, and Bruce H. Weber, "Evolution, Ethics, and the Complexity Revolution," *Evolution and Human Values*, edited by Robert Wesson and Patricia A. Williams (Rodipi, Amsterdam and Atlanta, GA, 1995), pp. 49 - 77.

KPMG has designed and implemented a risk-based strategic-systems auditing approach[2] called the Business Measurement Process, or BMP. The BMP audit approach has a top-down, holistic, business-risk orientation. It guides the focus, breadth and depth of the auditor's knowledge acquisition, and the integration of business knowledge into expectations about financial-statement assertions.

The traditional "risk-based" audit focuses the auditor's assessment of risk through a narrow "accounting lens" — a lens that directs his attention, and his related assessment and testing activities, to the nature of account balances, classes of transactions, and properties of the client's accounting system for the purpose of assessing the risk that financial-statement assertions are materially misstated. We believe that this disaggregative, "bottom-up" focus can inhibit the auditor's development of the level of business understanding needed to effectively judge financial-statement assertions. After all, these accounting and processing foci are "human artifacts" that are levels removed from the actual business activities to which they relate.

BMP has a very clear strategy focus. It is a risk-based strategic-systems audit approach that focuses the auditor's assessment of risk through a broader strategic-systems lens — a lens that directs the auditor's attention to the client's systems dynamics: its business strategy and the economic niches it has chosen to occupy; the strengths of its connections to outside economic agents, including customers, suppliers, investors, and regulators; and the external and internal forces that threaten the viability of its chosen niches and the achievement of its objectives. The BMP auditor collects and integrates information about the client's business and industry using a client business modeling[3] framework. The client business model assists the auditor's evaluation of the validity of the client's accounting transactions, and of the financial statements taken as a whole. Use of the top-down, aggrega-

---

2 The term "systems audit" is used elsewhere in the auditing literature as a label for a process with a focus on the client's accounting system, or some other internal system such as its regulatory compliance system. We use the label "strategic-systems lens" in this monograph to signify a process with a much broader perspective that grounds the auditor's risk assessment, testing, evaluation, and decision-making activities in a strategic-systems view of the client organization – a view that places the client at the core of a broader economic system that is an integrated whole, giving particular attention to the organization's strategies for maintaining and strengthening its fit within this broader system.

3 A business model is a knowledge-acquisition framework that guides the auditor's collection and integration of information about key attributes of the client's full economic system, including the external forces that bear upon an entity; the interlinking activities, or business processes, that are carried out within the entity; and the entity's relationships and interactions with persons and other organizations outside of the entity. KPMG has created a business modeling technology that assists the auditor's development of knowledge and evidence about these relationships and interactions for the purpose of conducting a financial-statement audit. The KPMG business modeling technology is described in more detail later in this monograph.

tive, strategic-systems lens increases the likelihood that the auditor will have obtained a sufficient understanding of the client's business and industry for the purpose of conducting a financial-statement audit, and reduces the risk that audit procedures applied to specific high-risk transactions will be prematurely truncated.

The purposes of this monograph are to present:

- an overview of the theories and trends that create a need for a risk-based strategic-systems audit;

- a discussion of the systems theory and strategy concepts that underly the risk-based strategic-systems audit;

- an overview of some of the business measurement principles, analytical procedures, and tools comprising KPMG's risk-based strategic-systems audit — BMP; and

- examples that illustrate how BMP might be applied to a retail client.

We begin the monograph by presenting an overview of current authoritative guidance about the auditor's need to understand the client's business and industry. Next, we present a brief historical overview of the role and practice of auditing prior to the late-nineteenth century, and of the influence of these past events and conditions on the evolution of auditing practices throughout the twentieth century. The historical perspective helps us to understand how and why audit practices have remained rather narrowly focused on transactions and other organizational sub-units over a period when the role of external auditing was expanding, and client businesses and the economy taken as a whole were becoming more complex.

Next, we discuss selected systems and strategy concepts relevant to the auditor's need to obtain an understanding of the client's business and industry, and to the manner in which he obtains that understanding. In this section we draw a distinction between the reductionist approach to audit risk assessment — assessing audit risk "through the accounting transactions" — and the strategic-systems approach — assessing audit risk through a top-down, holistic view of the client's business and its connections and interactions with its environment. We suggest that these perspectives are complements, and that the auditor should assess audit risk from both perspectives to make effective judgments about the validity of the client's financial statements in today's complex business environment.

Next, we present a proposed knowledge acquisition framework for the "whole-system" strategic approach for assessing audit risk, followed by a detailed discussion, with illustrations, of some of the business measurement principles and related analytical procedures comprising BMP — KPMG's current working version of such a framework. We conclude the monograph with a philosophical discussion about audit evidence as it relates to the strategic-systems-oriented analytical procedures.

2 Current Authoritative Guidance About the Need to Understand the Client's Business and Industry

The current authoritative guidance on external auditing addresses the key roles of judgment and an understanding of the client's business in the performance of the audit. But, such guidance says little about what constitutes an adequate breadth and depth of knowledge and the type of decision frame required to make sound professional audit judgments. Some relevant passages from the authoritative guidance dealing with judgment and business knowledge are presented in the appendix to this monograph. We excerpt from several passages below as we discuss the nature and focus of extant guidance on these matters.

AU Section 110 on *Responsibilities and Functions of the Independent Auditor* states: "In the observance of generally accepted auditing standards, the independent auditor must exercise his judgment in determining which auditing procedures are necessary in the circumstances to afford a reasonable basis for his opinion. His judgment is required to be the informed judgment of a qualified professional person" [AU 110.04, 1997].

Section 210 on *Training and Proficiency of the Independent Auditor* states:

> In the course of his day-to-day practice, the independent auditor encounters a wide range of judgment on the part of management, varying from true objective judgment to the occasional extreme of deliberate misstatement. He is retained to audit and report upon the financial statements of a business because, through his training and experience, he has become skilled in accounting and auditing and has acquired the ability to consider objectively and to exercise independent judgment with respect to the information recorded in books of account or otherwise disclosed by his audit [AU 210.05, 1997].

Sections 110 and 210 emphasize the need for, and role of, knowledge of accounting and auditing in the performance of the audit, but do not address the role of business knowledge in audit judgment and decision-making. Section 311 on *Planning and Supervision* discusses the auditor's need for knowledge of the client's business and industry:

> The nature, extent, and timing of planning vary with the size and complexity of the entity, experience with the entity, and knowledge of the entity's business [AU 311.03, 1997]. The auditor should

> obtain a level of knowledge of the entity's business that will enable him to plan and perform his audit in accordance with generally accepted auditing standards. That level of knowledge should enable him to obtain an understanding of the events, transactions, and practices that, in his judgment, may have a significant effect on the financial statements [AU 311.06, 1997].

AU Section 311 suggests that knowledge of the entity's business helps the auditor to evaluate the reasonableness of estimates and management representations, and helps the auditor to make difficult judgments about the appropriateness of the accounting principles applied by the client, and about the adequacy of disclosures in the client's financial statements. The passage from Section 311 presented below discusses the kind of knowledge the auditor should obtain, and the typical manner in which it is obtained.

> The auditor should obtain a knowledge of matters that relate to the nature of the entity's business, its organization, and its operating characteristics. Such matters include, for example, the type of business, types of products and services, capital structure, related parties, locations, and production, distribution, and compensation methods. The auditor should also consider matters affecting the industry in which the entity operates, such as economic conditions, government regulations, and changes in technology, as they relate to his audit. Other matters, such as accounting practices common to the industry, competitive conditions, and, if available, financial trends and ratios should also be considered by the auditor [AU 311.07, 1997]. Knowledge of an entity's business is ordinarily obtained through experience with the entity or its industry and inquiry of personnel of the entity [AU 311.08, 1997].

Finally, other sections of the authoritative guidance make passing references to the need for business knowledge when conducting a financial-statement audit. For example, Section 312 on *Audit Risk and Materiality in Conducting an Audit* states: "considerations of audit risk and materiality vary with the size and complexity of the entity, auditor's experience with the entity, and his knowledge of the entity's business" [AU 312.11, 1997]. And Section 341 on *The Auditor's Consideration of an Entity's Ability to Continue as a Going Concern* presents broad categories of conditions and events indicating that there could be a substantial doubt about the entity's ability to continue as a going concern for a reasonable period of time, such as negative trends, default on loans, internal work stoppages, legal proceedings, legislation, etc.

Our reading of the current authoritative guidance on the auditor's need to understand the client's business and industry supports the conclusion that it is more noteworthy for what is not stated than for what is stated. Clearly, some recognition is given to the auditor's need to understand the client's business. It is equally clear, however, that extant guidance does an inadequate job of explicating why such an understanding is necessary. As a consequence, guidance on the nature and extent of the auditor's knowledge, which provides the basis for that understanding, also is inadequate. More specifically, important questions are left unanswered, including:[4]

- Specifically, what business knowledge is needed, and to what level(s) of the client's business environment should the auditor direct his attention: industries; market niches; business strategies; financial strategies; business processes; business transactions; business control systems; etc.?

- How much knowledge about the client's business and industry is needed to obtain reasonable assurance that the assertions contained in the financial statements are not materially misstated?

- What is the relative importance of this business knowledge to the auditor's opinion, compared to the knowledge obtained about individual transactions, and what role should this knowledge play in the auditor's evaluation of individual transactions? Does knowledge about the client's business and industry constitute audit evidence?

---

4 We are not suggesting that the authoritative guidance should *specify* the extent and type of knowledge the auditor should obtain about the client's business and industry. These are matters that should be left to the auditor's professional judgment. What we are suggesting is that the authoritative guidance does not go deep enough to provide meaningful insights about these issues. Ultimately, concepts must be specified and labeled sufficiently to provide the auditor with useful guidance about the extent of his decision frame.

For example, we find no mention of the need to understand the client's strategy in the excerpts from the Statements on Auditing Standards (SAS's) presented in this monograph. The following passage from Palepu, Bernard, and Healy [1996, p. 1-2] suggests there is a clear linkage between a client's business strategy and the assertions embodied in its financial statements. "A firm's business activities are influenced by its economic environment and its own business strategy. . . . The firm's business strategy determines how the firm positions itself in its environment to achieve a competitive advantage. . . . [A] firm's financial statements summarize the economic consequences of its business activities." We believe the auditor needs to gain an understanding of the client's business strategy and related business objectives to develop valid expectations about the organization's performance. For example, the profit margin reported by a company whose strategy is to be a low-cost producer likely would not be expected to be significantly greater than its industry's average profit margin.

In the next section, we present a brief overview of the evolution of auditing practices in the United Kingdom and the United States. The historical perspective helps us to understand why today's authoritative guidance, and the types of actual procedures applied in contemporary practice of external auditing, are rather narrowly focused on accounting transactions and organizational sub-units, with less attention paid to the development of knowledge about the client's business and industry.

3 Overview of the Evolution of Auditing Practices

> *We must always remember . . . that the whole purpose of ancient accounting was not to measure the rate of profit or loss but to keep accurate records of acquisitions and outgoings, in money and kind, and to expose any losses due to dishonesty or negligence. This statement of the objectives of ancient accounting is also largely true of the system of "charge-and-discharge" accounting which developed in England. . . . Each of a hierarchy of officials had to account to his superior for incomings and outgoings on behalf of the owner of the estate. . . . The accounts were the basis of the periodic audit. . . . Although the early profit-and-loss account yielded a figure of periodic profit, its determination was in many ways subordinate and subservient to the statement of asset "value" in the ledger.*

> B. S. Yamey
>
> *Some Topics in the History of Financial Accounting in England, 1500-1900*[5]

Throughout its history, the practice of auditing has been tied to the needs of the day and to the system of accounting that served those needs. Yamey,[6] in his article about the major features of double-entry bookkeeping as practiced in the United Kingdom during the sixteenth through the nineteenth centuries, describes the nature of accounting user needs and related accounting practices during the period in which the forerunners to the modern-day corporation were emerging. He suggests [p. 11] that "The origins of accounting and indeed of written records are probably to be found in the need of an 'accounting' officer to render a statement of money and other assets received in his charge on behalf of his employer, or disbursed on his behalf. There was a need for a check on the honesty and reliability of subordinates." Consistently, Watts and Zimmerman,[7] in their study of the history of audits conducted for the English guilds as early as 1200, suggest that audits were performed by guild members to monitor manager's contracts. Watts and Zimmerman [p. 618] state that "It [the

---

5 B. S. Yamey, "Some Topics in the History of Financial Accounting in England, 1500-1900" reprinted in *Studies in Accounting*, edited by W. T. Baxter and S. Davidson(The Institute of Chartered Accountants, 1977) pp. 11 - 34.
6 *Ibid.* Yamey's observations were based on his review of the surviving account-books of nine prominent English businessmen, and an obscure seventeenth-century merchant.
7 R. L. Watts and J. L. Zimmerman, "Agency Problems, Auditing, and the Theory of the Firm: Some Evidence," *Journal of Law and Economics*, 1983, pp. 613-633.

audit] came at the end of the managers' tenure and was designed to check for unauthorized expenditures. Further, it also appears to have been designed to check for other breaches of contracts."

Prior to 1900, the audit addressed the need for an independent check on the accounting for stocks and flows, and served as an additional mechanism for motivating honest and reliable behavior of subordinates or stewards who were entrusted with the possession and use of someone else's assets. The auditor would perform a variety of tasks including observing the physical existence of reported assets in the possession of the steward, verifying their ownership through inspection of supporting documents, and assessing the accuracy of their reported values (usually costs) using knowledge of the business or through inquiries made to external parties. By "counting" the stock on hand at a given point in time, both in money and in kind, and then comparing these amounts with those determined during the preceding audit, or those for assets originally entrusted under the care of the steward when no prior audit had been performed, the independent auditor could articulate the changes in his counts with subordinates' accountings of acquisitions and outgoings.

The business knowledge required to perform this "balance sheet audit" would have included a basic understanding of bookkeeping methods and procedures, knowledge of the nature of the business' activities, and knowledge of the costs and market values of the goods traded by merchants or safeguarded and used by stewards.

As the nineteenth century was drawing to a close, accounting and auditing were about to enter a period of rapid change. Western civilization was moving from the agricultural age into the industrial age. Machines were being invented that enabled mass production of food, other crops (e.g., cotton), and other goods and services. Other machines were invented, e.g., the steam engine, the locomotive, the automobile, and the telephone, that increased the speed and quality of human transportation and communication. These inventions increased individuals' mobility, which consequently drove the scale and complexity of business organizations to a higher level.

Concurrently, equity investment began to be widely used as a source of capital for these larger and more complex business organizations,[8] creat-

---

8 Yamey credits the rapid growth in importance of joint stock companies as the primary motivation for the development and practice of profit measurement in nineteenth-century England. Profits represented an upper limit on dividend payments to shareholders and provided a means for absentee shareholders to monitor the performance of their investments. Yamey [*Ibid.*, p. 26] writes "To a large extent they had to rely for their impressions of the success and soundness of their company on information made available by the active management. The periodic profit figure not unnaturally came to be regarded as an indicator of the profitability of operations, a summary of the results of the interaction of numerous business decisions and economic circumstances of which the shareholders had no detailed knowledge."

ing the need for new kinds of financial information, and a new approach to auditing. Equity investors began demanding information about the earning power of their investments, and the periodic profit figure became important as an index of profitability and began being reported to both current and potential shareholders. As a result of these changing user needs and the new accounting conventions developed to serve these needs, the role of the external audit expanded from a check for unauthorized expenditures by management, or a check for dishonesty of subordinates, to a check on the representational faithfulness of a company's reported profit and financial position.

An early edition of Montgomery's book on *Auditing Theory and Practice* [1912] made a distinction between the two kinds of audits that served these different user needs: (1) the detailed audit, which prevailed in the formative days of auditing in America and for which the objectives were the detection or prevention of fraud and errors; and (2) the audit designed to ascertain the actual financial condition and earnings of an enterprise for its partners, stockholders, executives, bankers, or investors. According to Montgomery, the latter represented a "vastly broader and more important class of work" that relegated the objectives of detailed audits "to a subordinate position without in any way depreciating their importance."[9]

In the United States throughout the first half of the twentieth century, new accounting concepts and principles were developed to accommodate expanding user needs for information about the financial performance of business organizations. In addition, in 1913 the United States Congress passed the income tax law, which provided additional impetus for the development and refinement of methods to account for profit and loss. Although advances were being made in the area of income measurement, auditing methods used in practice continued to focus on the balance sheet. For example, during the early twentieth century, bankers in the United States reinforced the balance-sheet audit focus by beginning to ask commercial loan applicants to submit balance sheets signed by auditors.[10]

Throughout the twentieth century, as organizations grew larger and became more complex in other ways (e.g., expanding absentee ownership, vertical and horizontal integration, etc.), auditors adapted by changing

9 Timothy B. Bell and Arnold M. Wright, eds., *Auditing Practice, Research, and Education: A Productive Collaboration* (AICPA, 1995), pp. 15 and 16.
10 Chapter 2 from Bell and Wright [*Ibid.*] by Barry E. Cushing, Lynford E. Graham, Jr., Zoe-Vanna Palmrose, Robert S. Roussey, and Ira Solomon reports [p. 18] that "the first authoritative pronouncement on auditing in America was the 'Memorandum on Balance-Sheet Audits' prepared in 1917 by the AIA at the request of the Federal Trade Commission. This pronouncement was issued by the Federal Reserve Board in 1918 under the title *Approved Methods for the Preparation of Balance Sheet Statements*."

from exhaustive testing of reported acquisitions and outgoings to selective testing of accounting transactions. Consistently, they invented what sometimes is called a risk-based audit approach[11] whereby the auditor would look to the nature of individual transactions, e.g., transactions whose dollar value exceeded a size threshold, the nature of account balances and whole classes of transactions, and to qualities of the client's accounting system to form preliminary judgments about the risk of material misstatements for the purpose of planning the focus and scope of tests of details work. And, auditors used the concept of materiality to define their testing domain and the limits of their responsibility as independent attesters.

Clearly, contemporary audit approaches incorporate numerous advances. But today one key aspect of the early balance-sheet audit remains relatively unchanged — the auditor's risk assessment and testing foci continue to be oriented primarily toward "counting" of organizational sub-units, and testing of individual transactions. The financial-statement assertions of primary concern to the auditor in risk assessment, and given the most attention in today's authoritative auditing pronouncements — existence/occurrence, completeness, rights and obligations, valuation or allocation, and presentation and disclosure — are made at the individual transaction level, or at the class of transactions or account balance levels.

As the global economy, the business organizations operating within it, and organizations' business strategies become increasingly complex and interdependent,[12] we believe more attention should be paid to the development of auditing methods and procedures that focus on assertions at the entity-level — methods and procedures that promise greater power to detect material misstatements as they allow the auditor to ground key judgments in a more critical and holistic understanding of the client's systems dynamics. We further believe that today's complex economic world requires a break from the auditing traditions that have evolved from the early balance-sheet audit — traditions under which the auditor's attention is focused primarily at the sub-unit level, and his views about what is evidence are heavily skewed toward tangibility (i.e., the physical existence of assets, the existence of tangible documentation supporting transactions, etc.).

---

11 A risk-based approach to auditing has been defined as "a systematic approach in which the nature, timing, and extent of testing are determined by assessing and evaluating the risk that financial-statement assertions are materially misstated" (Bell and Wright, *Ibid.*, p. 11).

12 Both G. Hamel and C. K. Prahalad (*Competing for the Future* [Harvard Business School Press, Boston, 1994]) and A. Brandenburger and B. Nalebuff (*Co-Opetition* [The Free Press, New York, 1996]) discuss the impacts of global competition on competitive strategies and the ever-increasing use of strategic alliances in global competition.

Today's auditor should place more weight on knowledge about the client's business and industry, and its interactions with its environment, when forming an opinion about the validity of financial-statement assertions. Also, we believe that financial-statement assertions about entity-level strategic performance are just as important, if not more important, than assertions about organizational sub-units. Further, we believe the knowledge acquisition and decision processes required to develop valid expectations about these broader assertions are different from the processes required to test assertions at the sub-unit level.

In the next section, we review concepts from the fields of systems theory and strategy that speak to the importance of obtaining an understanding of the client's business strategy and systems dynamics for the purpose of conducting a financial-statement audit. We present the case that the perspective, or lens, through which the auditor makes his assessment of audit risk will impact his ability to effectively evaluate financial-statement assertions and we propose the use of a broader, "whole-system" strategic lens for assessing audit risk as we move into the twenty-first century.

4 Assessing Audit Risk Through a Strategic-Systems Lens

The reductionist description of organisms can be useful and may in some cases be necessary. It is dangerous only when it is taken to be the complete explanation. Reductionsim and holism, analysis and synthesis, are complementary approaches that, used in proper balance, help us obtain a deeper knowledge. . . .

From the systems point of view the unit of survival is not an entity at all, but rather a pattern of organization adopted by an organism in its interactions with its environment. . . .

Fritjof Capra
The Turning Point[13]

A *system* is a collection of parts that interact to function as a whole. The behavior of a system depends on its entire structure, the relative strengths of the many connections among its parts at any point in time, and the manner and degree to which these connections change over time. Systems theory involves the study of living systems as integrated wholes whose emergent properties cannot be reduced to those of smaller sub-units. Viewed from a systems perspective, the world consists of relationships and integration. Instead of concentrating on basic building blocks to learn about the properties of the larger system, the systems approach emphasizes basic principles of organization — how the parts are interrelated and coordinated into a unified whole. From that viewpoint, value-creating strategies emerge through learning and only can be understood by analyzing the system conditions that give rise to success and strategy innovation.[14] We firmly believe that today's financial-statement auditor should assess client business risk and audit risk from a "strategic-systems" perspective.[15]

---

[13] Fritjof Capra, *The Turning Point — Science, Society, and the Rising Culture* (Bantam Books, New York, 1982), pp. 267-268.

[14] G. Hamel and C. K. Prahalad in *Competing for the Future* (Harvard Business School Press, Boston, 1994) define strategy in the following terms: "Strategy is both a process of understanding and shaping competitive forces and a process of open-minded discovery and purposeful incrementalism."

[15] For a range of views of strategy consistent with the systems view see K. R. Andrews, *The Concept of Corporate Strategy* (Dow Jones-Irwin, New York, 1971); R. Ackoff, *The Democratic Corporation* (Oxford University Press, New York 1992); and G. Hamel, "Strategy As Revolution," *Harvard Business Review* (July/Aug 1996).

From the systems theorist's perspective, a living system interacts with its environment through *structural coupling* — recurring interactions, each of which triggers structural changes in the system, such as when a cell membrane infuses substances from its environment into its metabolic processes, or when an organism's central nervous system changes its connectivity after receiving information. A structurally-coupled system is a learning system. The structure of such a system continually changes in response to its environment. Consequently, adaptation, learning, and development are key characteristics of the behavior of living systems.

The Organization as a Complex Living System

Similar to other living systems, a business organization is a common purpose *superorganism*[16] whose productivity, profitability, adaptability, and ultimate survival are dependent on the strength of its intra- and interconnections — structural couplings and symbiotic alliances among the business processes comprising the organization itself, and between the organization and external economic agents.

Client business risk — the risk that an entity's business objectives will not be attained as a result of the external and internal factors, pressures, and forces brought to bear on the entity and, ultimately, the risk associated with the entity's survival and profitability — can be viewed from a systems perspective in terms of the strengths of the connections between an organization's strategies and business processes and its external environment. That is, any external or internal force that threatens to weaken an organization's connections to its external environment poses a business risk.[17] For example, *Internal Control – Integrated Framework* (Committee of

---

16 William Wheeler wrote in his 1911 essay entitled "The Ant Colony as an Organism," published in the *Journal of Morphology*, that an insect colony is not merely the analog of an organism, it is indeed an organism, in every important and scientific sense of the word. Wheeler called the tightly interconnected insect colony a "superorganism," to distinguish it from an organism that appears to the human eye to be a self-contained, single living unit. Similarly, a business organization is a living organism in every sense of the word. For a discussion of the view of the organization as a living system, see Arie De Geus, *The Living Company* (Harvard Business School Press, Boston, 1997).

17 Client business risk is conceptually similar to state-defined strategic risk as discussed in the strategy literature. Specifically, in *Strategic Risk: A State-Defined Approach* (Kluwer Academic Publishers, Norwell, MA, 1996), James Collins and Tim Ruefli (p. 56) suggest that "The strategic risk for an individual firm can be defined in terms of: (1) the probability of a firm moving from its present category to a lower ranked category, and (2) the magnitude of that move." Collins and Ruefli's categories are ordered groupings based on longitudinal data for a reference set of firms. To illustrate, firm performance over time may be measured on some dimension (e.g., ROI or customer satisfaction for each year in the present decade) for all firms in an industry. The reference group (i.e., the firms in the industry including the client organization) can be broken into categories (e.g., quartiles). Continuing this illustration, the state-defined risk for a client organization would be a function of the probability of moving from the first quartile of the ROI or customer satisfaction distribution to a lower category (e.g., second, third, or fourth quartiles).

Sponsoring Organizations of the Treadway Commission, 1992, 1994), Vol 1, p. 33, states that "Risks affect each entity's ability to survive; successfully compete within its industry; maintain its financial strength and positive public image; and maintain the overall quality of its products, services and people."

Like the cell membrane, the human central nervous system, and other open systems, organizations develop within themselves sophisticated mediating processes that intervene between external forces and organizational behavior. At higher levels of complexity, these mediating processes become more independent and autonomous and more determinative of the organization's interactions with its environment (e.g., consider the recent trend toward employee empowerment).

At the entity level, organizations exhibit emergent behavior — that is, they behave quite differently from how they would behave if their sub-units were independent of each other. According to Kees van der Heijden,[18] a retired executive from Royal Dutch/Shell who headed their Business Environment Division and was in charge of scenario planning:

> Emergent behavior is the outside behavioral manifestation of the internal mediating processes. In systems terms it implies a hierarchical organization, with the upper level guiding and constraining the actions at the lower. It is the constraints on the lower level members that creates the emergent behavior at the higher level. . . . If such constraints did not exist, lower level members would carry on as if they were independent, and there would be no emergent behavior, and therefore no identity for the larger system.[19]

The level of complexity inherent in an organization is a characteristic of the system's structure, and is impacted by the total number of its individual sub-units, the number of different layers in the structural hierarchy, the number of different business processes that perform business activities, and the number and strengths of connections among all of these sub-units, and between these sub-units and outside economic agents.

Stafford Beer, a British operations researcher, has studied and written extensively about how to model the dynamics of complex systems like today's business organizations. Beer places such structures as brains

---

18 Kees Van der Heijden, *Scenarios: The Art of Strategic Conversation* (John Wiley & Sons Ltd., Chichester, West Sussex, England, 1996), p. 39.
19 For example, in the aggregate, markets exhibit different behaviors than the individuals trading within them.

national economies, and corporations in a class of systems he calls "exceedingly complex." In his book *Brain of the Firm: The Managerial Cybernetics of Organization*,[20] Beer presents a five-level hierarchy of components of any viable system, modeled after the human nervous system. A summarized version of Beer's hierarchy is presented in Exhibit 1.[21] We have added the right-hand column in Exhibit 1 to depict our view of what are the business analogs of the hierarchical levels comprising the human nervous system.

According to Richardson:[22]

> In Beer's view every viable system is organized in such a hierarchy of five systems. Furthermore, complex viable systems are composed of viable subsystems that again have this five-level structure. To be viable, a division of a firm should be organized this way. The entire firm as a set of interrelated divisions should also have the same sort of structure. A viable sector of an economy should have the same structure. Naturally, an entire national economy, to be viable, should be similarly organized. Viewed from the elevated level of the national economy, in the hierarchy an individual firm or sector

Exhibit 1
Beer's Hierarchy of Components of a Viable System

System Level	Physical Analog	Function	Business Analog
System One	Organ, Muscle	Action	Business Processes
System Two	Spinal Cord	Signal Processing and Transmission	Information Systems
System Three	Pons/Medulla	Autonomic Control	Controls Embedded in Business Processes
System Four	Diencephalon, Ganglia	Monitoring the System and Its Environment; Sensing; Arousing Systems Three and Five	Risk Management Process
System Five	Cortex	Policy Formation	Strategic Management Process

---

20 Stafford Beer, *Brain of the Firm: The Managerial Cybernetics of Organization* (John Wiley and Sons, Chicester, 1981).
21 Taken from George P. Richardson, *Feedback Thought in Social Science and Systems Theory* (University of Pennsylvania Press, Philadelphia, 1991), p. 187.
22 *Ibid.*, p. 186.

operates at the level of systems one, two and three. The functions of its own high-level systems four and five are seen as part of the autonomic processes of the more aggregate system.

As discussed in later sections in this monograph, using the KPMG Business Measurement Process the auditor analyzes each of the five system levels (business analogs) presented in Exhibit 1, and integrates these analyses with other analyses of the client's environment, to form his "whole-system" decision frame for the assessment of the validity of financial-statement assertions.

The Strategic-Systems Lens

To gain the appropriate level of understanding of a client's business and industry for the purpose of conducting a financial-statement audit, we believe that today's auditor should direct his attention to the client's systems dynamics — its strategic positioning within its environment; its emergent behaviors that impact its attained level of performance; the strength of its connections, or structural couplings, to outside economic agents; the nature and impact of any symbiotic alliances; the specific interrelationships and internal process interactions that dominate its performance; and potential changes in other reaches of the vast economic web that might threaten the viability of the client's strategies and niches. These systemic properties determine the strategic competencies and capabilities[23] that enhance the value of the organization and that promote changes in that value over time.

We further believe that the perspective, or mental orientation — that is, the lens itself — through which the auditor obtains knowledge about the client's business and industry, and through which he considers client business risk and assesses audit risk, will influence his audit judgments and actions. Financial statements, and the accounting principles that have been developed to produce them, are designed to provide a valid portrayal of the client's systems dynamics — interactions comprising a broader economic system that, for the purpose of financial reporting, has the client organization at its core. The external auditor runs the risk of drawing incorrect inferences about the validity of the client's financial statements if he were to lose sight of the fact that the audit effectively is an assessment of the strength of interrelationships and interactions comprising this

---

23 For a review of the theory of competence-based competition see C. K. Prahalad and G. Hamel "The Core Competence of the Corporation," *Harvard Business Review* (May/June 1990), pp. 79 - 91; D. J. Collins and C. A. Montgomery, "Competing on Resources: Strategy in the 1990s," *Harvard Business Review* (July/Aug 1995), pp. 118 - 125; G. Stalk, Jr., P. Evans, and L. E. Shulman, "Competing on Capabilities: The New Rules of Corporate Strategy," *Harvard Business Review* (Mar/Apr 1992), pp. 51 - 68; and R. Sanchez, A. Heene, and H. Thomas, *The Theory of Competence-Based Competition* (Elsevier, New York, 1996).

broader economic system. In a sense, it is this broader system that is actually being "audited."

Exhibit 2 depicts an audit client as a complex web of interrelationships
embedded within a broader complex economic web.[24] The Exhibit 2 field
of view is what the auditor sees when he looks through the strategic-systems lens. The strengths of the many interrelationships comprising this
broader economic web reflect the extent of the organization's ability to
create value and generate the cash flow needed to sustain growth. A fundamental understanding of the strengths of these connections will provide
a basis for development of expectations about the quality and creativity of
the entity's strategies and its attained level of performance.

We are not suggesting that the traditional external auditor does not direct his
attention to many of these relationships. One-off procedures like tracking
industry trends, confirming receivables, reviewing and testing related-party
transactions, etc., do address the strengths of relationships between the
client and its external environment. What we are suggesting is subtle and
yet, in our view, a perspective that is much more powerful — that the auditor should consider the broader economic system depicted in Exhibit 2 as
an integrated whole. Further, we are suggesting that to effectively "audit"
this broader system, the auditor needs to establish a work process that

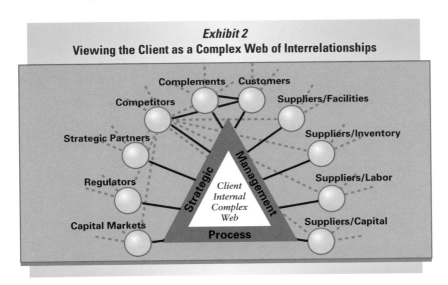

Exhibit 2
Viewing the Client as a Complex Web of Interrelationships

Complements   Customers
Competitors   Suppliers/Facilities
Strategic Partners   Suppliers/Inventory
Strategic   Management
Regulators   Client Internal Complex Web   Suppliers/Labor
Capital Markets   Process   Suppliers/Capital

---

24 Client organizations similarly have been characterized as a nexus of contracts within the academic literature. See, for example, James. A. Brickley, Clifford W. Smith, and Jerold L. Zimmerman, *Organizational
Architecture: A Managerial Economics Approach* (Richard D. Irwin, New York, 1996).

places more weight on developing knowledge about, and evidence in support of, the strengths of its interconnections, the rapidity and magnitude of changes in its connectivity, and the viability of the firm's strategies.

As with any adaptive system, the strength of these connections will change over time. For example, assume that the organization depicted in Exhibit 2 is a retail bookseller with a heavy capital investment in retail facilities located around the country. Now, assume that a new market niche emerges, involving the use of the World Wide Web, in lieu of retail outlets, to market and sell books. New competitors occupying this niche offer access to much larger inventories than any retail outlet can stock, and can price their books at a substantial discount because of lower overhead costs. In addition, consumers can search these massive inventories using search engines provided by the new competitors, and can access book reviews by other consumers available through these competitors' Web sites.

As the number of consumers connected to the World Wide Web grows over time, the connections between customers and competitors occupying this new niche are likely to increase in number. And, in turn, unless it adapts its own operation by moving into this new niche, the strength of connections between the original retailer and most of the other economic agents depicted in Exhibit 2 will diminish. For example, as the original retailer experiences a drop in demand, it will respond by reducing its own demand for facilities, inventory, labor, and capital.[25]

Pitfalls of the Transactions Lens — The LSL Case Study

Traditionally, auditors have assessed audit risk and tested significant accounting transactions using a transactions lens. As with a camera lens, a

---

[25] Amazon.com, a bookseller that markets and sells books exclusively on the World Wide Web, advertises an inventory of 2.5 million titles, and claims that the largest physical bookstore offers only about 175,000 books. During May 1997, Barnes and Noble filed suit against Amazon.com, alleging that their claim to be the largest bookstore is false advertising. Announcement of the suit came right around the time that Amazon.com went public with an initial stock offering. Bruce Guptill, an analyst at the Gartner Group, was quoted as having said that "the lawsuit will most likely be thrown out. It's a publicity thing." Barnes and Noble announced a strategic alliance with America On-Line around the same time, under which AOL users can link to Barnes and Noble's book-ordering Web site. Also during May 1997, a *Wall Street Journal* article entitled "Bookstore Survival Stunts Have Scant Literary Merit" reported that "the independents continue to lose ground to book superstores. . . . Last year, total retail volume rose about 3% to 1.06 billion books sold, but independents' share slid to an estimated 19% from 25% five years ago, according to the Book Industry Study Group."

The example presented here is not intended to suggest that any existing book retailer is likely to go out of business. Our purpose is to illustrate to the reader, through a hypothetical example, how the strengths of connections between businesses and outside economic agents are in a state of constant flux, just like all living systems, and that viewing an audit client through a strategic-systems lens can shift the auditor's focus in such a way that he can gain additional insights about the client's business and industry that can enhance his performance of the audit.

transactions lens frames the assessment within a narrow or limited field of view. Instead of focusing the auditor's attention on the broad business context surrounding the transactions, and the role of the transactions within that context, the transactions lens more narrowly focuses his attention on the transactions as stand-alone events, thereby increasing the risk that the auditor might misconstrue their context, meaning, or purpose. Also, with the transactions orientation there can be an associated tendency to become overly preoccupied with the mechanics of the accounting afforded the transaction, with insufficient attention being paid to its economic underpinnings. A narrow focus on the mechanics of the accounting can divert the auditor's attention from making important considerations about the roles transactions play in the achievement of the entity's strategic objectives.

A recent study of the audit procedures applied to a small number of highly significant real-estate transactions in the audits of Lincoln Savings and Loan (LSL) during 1986 and 1987[26] suggests simultaneously that a transactions risk-assessment orientation can be problematic and that a comprehensive client business model might be a more effective decision frame for evaluating significant transactions. Viewed through a traditional-audit transactions lens, the LSL auditor would focus on questions like (1) Are the loan loss reserves adequate? (2) Are gains on securities "real" and recorded properly? (3) Are gains on sales of undeveloped land "real" and recorded properly? Considering (3) in more detail, for example, the traditional auditor would ask: Do terms of the land sales meet the criteria set forth in SFAS No. 66 for use of the full accrual revenue recognition accounting method? Further, the SFAS No. 66 revenue recognition criteria would direct the traditional auditor to factors such as the required percentage down payment and the required repayment terms.

When a team of professors recently examined the performance of the LSL auditor, they concluded that the application of analytical procedures to the economic substance of LSL's significant raw-land-sales transactions was inadequate. "What we judge to be weaknesses were not due to under sampling of transactions or a highly technical misapplication of audit procedures, but rather weaknesses in the application of a basic tenet of auditing — obtaining and integrating an understanding of the economics of the client's business with other audit evidence." These researchers also concluded that "the auditor's transactions approach to the audit appears to have inhibited their consideration of the economic reasonableness of transactions.

---

26 Merle M. Erickson, Brian W. Mayhew, and William L. Felix, Jr., "Understanding the Client's Business: Lessons from Lincoln Savings and Loan," unpublished working paper (1996).

The transactions level focus supported full revenue recognition on most of LSL's major raw land sales during 1986-87. The analysis on a sample of material transactions indicates that a detailed understanding of LSL's business could have led to different revenue recognition conclusions."

To elaborate on the researchers' conclusions, consider what might have happened if the LSL auditor had constructed a comprehensive client business model and focused on developing an understanding of client business risk before auditing the significant land-sales transactions. This auditor might pose the same initial questions (1) - (3), yet focus in on (3) by asking the following question: How can an entity sell recently purchased, remotely located, undeveloped land at prices amounting to 400-500% above cost in the economic climate in which LSL was operating? Importantly, this auditor would be looking for evidence of strategic and process advantage and would juxtapose the question against the following considerations about LSL's current business environment:[27]

- *Current Economic Climate* — The Arizona residential real estate market was declining; there were decreasing construction awards, a decreasing rate in the number of home building permits issued, and there was a negative population migration trend. The Arizona press had reported an overall decline in the real estate industry;

- *Regulatory Changes* — The federal government substantially deregulated the S&L industry allowing expansion of the assets of S&Ls into areas other than home mortgages. In addition, the *Tax Reform Act of 1986* significantly reduced the tax benefits for real estate investment;

- *Disputes With Regulators* — Regulators asserted that LSL had violated direct investment rules. Regulators also were concerned about LSL's unorthodox business practices, including its large junk bond portfolio and loose underwriting practices;

- *Strategic Reorientation* — LSL changed from a traditional S&L to a real estate investment speculator; LSL expanded its real estate inventory; LSL relied on a small number of large transactions to generate its profits; and LSL changed its investment strategy, moving into high-risk securities;

- *Auditor Resignation* — The 8-K filed with the SEC cites Arthur Andersen's concerns over the FHLB's disagreements with some of LSL's policies; and

---

27 According to Erickson et al. [1996], all of these conditions and events could have been, or were, known by the LSL auditor prior to signing his opinion on the 1987 LSL financial statements.

- *LSL's Current Performance* — LSL's interest spreads were very thin and not enough to cover provisions for losses. There also were significant non-routine transactions — the main source of profits for 1986-87 were sales of undeveloped land. LSL's book equity approached the minimum capital threshold set by regulators.

We believe that these factors and considerations strongly suggest a "they can't" answer to the question, How can LSL sell recently purchased, remotely located, undeveloped land at prices amounting to 400-500% above cost, given the economic climate in which LSL was operating? LSL had no apparent strategic or process advantage that would compensate for the negatives revealed by the LSL business model. Further, the implications of the "they can't" answer likely would not be lost on an auditor viewing LSL through a strategic-systems lens instead of a transactions lens. The systemic properties recounted above indicate significant weaknesses in the relationships between LSL and outside economic agents. Would the outcome of the LSL audit have been different if the auditor placed LSL at the center of Exhibit 2, and developed a full-blown business model, giving explicit consideration to the strengths of the connections between LSL and these outside economic agents?

Perhaps the greatest challenge an external auditor faces during a period of rapid change is to develop an understanding of the implications of recent "shocks" to the economic system within which the client operates, and to anticipate the speed with which such shocks will impact his client's profitability and survival. With hindsight, it is easy for us to see that certain shocks to the economic system in which LSL operated — namely the *Tax Reform Act of 1986*, and deregulation of the S&L industry — had a significant impact on the strengths of connections between LSL and its environment. However, it appears that this broader economic system swiftly changed its connectivity, i.e., economic agents adapted to the economic shocks very rapidly. For example, just prior to the 1986–87 period, the Arizona residential real estate market had experienced dramatic growth.

We are not suggesting here that the LSL auditor's expectations about the legitimacy of LSL's land sales were irrational. Clearly, the LSL auditor was not the only auditor at that time that was affected by the speed with which economic shocks negatively impacted the real estate market and cascaded through the S&L industry. Virtually no Big-6 firm emerged from this period of economic adjustment unscathed. What we are suggesting is that the transactions lens through which those expectations were developed may have inhibited the auditor's ability to understand the extent and speed of the economic adjustments taking place. A broader strategic-systems lens that would have focused his attention more directly on the broader economic system's adaptive behavior might have increased his level of skepticism about the reasonableness of reported gains, and consequently led to the development of more accurate expectations.

We believe that today's financial-statement auditor should gain an understanding of the systemic properties of the client's operating environment, including the nature and effectiveness of the interactions among its internal business processes and its external environment. We call this a *risk-based strategic-systems audit* — an audit involving two complementary foci: a holistic focus to understand and evaluate the client's strategic-systems dynamics, and a reductionist focus involving evaluation of its detailed transactions from a grounding in knowledge about their larger systems context.

A systems view of the organization challenges us to consider its broadest business context and to ground our inferences about properties of its parts, e.g., its business activities, business processes, and individual accounting transactions, in a comprehensive understanding of this broader strategic context.

In the next section, we discuss some of the possible shocks arising from changes in the global business environment that should be considered by the auditor as he develops expectations about the viability of an organization's strategies, and its attained level of performance and financial condition.

5 The Global Business Environment

The goods and services in an economic web exist only because each is useful in either the fabrication or the creation of another good or service, as an intermediate good, or is useful to some ultimate consumer. Goods and services "live" in niches created by other goods and services. The mutualism of the biosphere, where advantages of trade exist, finds its mirror in economic systems, where advantages of trade exist in the vast web of goods and services.

Stuart Kauffman
At Home in the Universe: The Search for the Laws of Self-Organization and Complexity[28]

Organizations occupy niches afforded by what others do and their ability to create value depends on the needs and wants of others, and the strength of their connections to these outsiders. Because the web of technologies is interconnected, the extinction of one good or service can initiate an avalanche in which other goods and services no longer make sense and lapse from view. The advent of the automobile is an example of such a shock to the broad economic system. For example, Kauffman [1995, p. 279] states:

> The car comes in and drives the horse out. When the horse goes, so does the smithy, the saddlery, the stable, the harness shop, buggies, and in your West, out goes the Pony Express. But once cars are around, it makes sense to expand the oil industry, build gas stations dotted over the countryside, and pave the roads. Once the roads are paved, people start driving all over creation, so motels make sense. What with the speed, traffic lights, traffic cops, traffic courts, and the quiet bribe to get off your parking ticket make their way into the economy and our behavior patterns.

Organizations have visions and missions[29] that provide the basis for their business objectives. To achieve these objectives, the organization sets strategies, designs and implements processes, and acquires and uses resources.

---

28 Stuart Kauffman, *At Home in the Universe: The Search for the Laws of Self-Organization and Complexity* (Oxford University Press, New York, Oxford, 1995), pp. 191-192. Kauffman is a leader in the field of complexity theory.
29 For a thorough discussion of these concepts, see J. C. Collins and J. I. Porras, *Built to Last: Successful Habits of Visionary Companies* (HarperCollins, New York, 1994); A. Campbell, M. Devine and D. Young, *A Sense of Mission* (Economist Books, 1990); and G. Hamel and C. K. Prahalad, "Strategic Intent," *Harvard Business Review* (May/June, 1989), pp. 63 - 76.

Rapid strategic reorientation is required when strategies become less viable, or else the organization's survival is jeopardized. To make sound professional judgments about assertions embodied in the financial statements, the auditor needs to understand the client's current strategy and its process for adapting its strategy to changing environmental conditions and emerging business risks.

In the past, managers perceived that the local markets in which their organizations sold their goods and services were their organizations' economic domains. Risk management focused on environmental changes within these local domains. This limited focus was acceptable for strategic planning purposes in the mid-twentieth century industrial era when barriers to entry were substantial. During that period, regional markets were separated by long distances, transportation was neither abundant nor cheap, and technologies were not easily replicable.

During the twentieth century, technological advances in transportation and communication have opened the way for the interconnection of economic agents into vastly more complex economic webs. These technologies compress distance and time, making individuals and organizations more nimble and also more interdependent. The compression of distance and time intensifies competition by presenting new business opportunities to competitors through access to world markets, and by enabling the rapid learning of competitors' technologies, which reduces barriers to entry. Dee Hock, founder of Visa International, characterizes this latter information age phenomenon as the *disappearance of scientific float* — the time between the invention of a new technology and its universal application. For example, Hock recounts that it took centuries for information about the smelting process to cross a continent and bring on the Iron Age. It took decades for the steam engine, electric light, and automobile to attain universal acceptance. It was only a matter of years after their invention that radio and television gained widespread use. Hock comments: "Today, countless devices utilizing microchips sweep around the earth like the light of the sun into universal, instant use."[30]

In today's world, distance is no longer a barrier to market entry, technologies are rapidly replicated by competitors, and information and communi-

---

30 Dee W. Hock, "Institutions in the Age of Mindcrafting," presented at the Bionomics Annual Conference, San Francisco, October 22, 1994. Reproduced with permission by Cascade Policy Institute, and accessible from their Web site, "www.cascadepolicy.org/dee_hock.htm."

cations technologies are shaping a new economic order. To manage their business risks effectively, organizations must now view their playing field as the whole global economy.[31]

Exhibit 3 depicts the global business environment within which organizations now operate and coevolve, and in which new organizational forms such as strategic alliances, global consortia, electronic commerce, and the like are constantly emerging. The concentric circles represent a hierarchy of three environmental layers. Examples of business risks arising from these three environments also are presented in Exhibit 3.

Prudent managers continually scan the following three environments for indications of the emergence of business risks that threaten the attainment of their business objectives — the organization's internal environment; the local external operating environment; and the broader global business

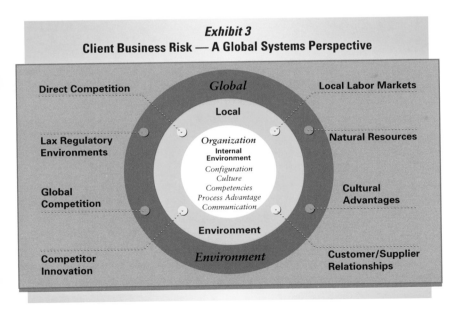

Exhibit 3
Client Business Risk — A Global Systems Perspective

Direct Competition · *Global* · Local Labor Markets

Local

Lax Regulatory Environments · *Organization* Internal Environment · Natural Resources

Configuration
Culture
Global Competition · *Competencies* *Process Advantage* *Communication* · Cultural Advantages

Environment

Competitor Innovation · *Environment* · Customer/Supplier Relationships

---

31 For thorough discussions of the "shocks" created by globalization, see G. Hamel and C. K. Prahalad, *Competing for the Future* (Harvard Business School Press, Boston, 1994); M. E. Porter, *Competitive Advantage of Nations* (The Free Press, New York, 1990); Ohmae, K., *The Borderless World: Power and Strategy in the Intelligent Economy* (HarperCollins, New York, 1990); and J. Hagel, III, and A. G. Armstrong, *Net Gain: Expanding Markets Through Virtual Communities* (Harvard Business School Press, Boston, 1997).

environment. The associated business risks arise from:

- conditions and forces within the organization's internal environment;
- industry forces; and
- macroenvironmental forces.

The core shown in Exhibit 3 represents the organization's internal environment. Some risks that can arise in an organization's internal environment are:

- *an improper organizational configuration* — increasing organizational complexity challenges existing organizational structures, e.g., strategies and core business processes might be misaligned because of a functional management orientation and stovepiped organizational configuration;

- *a dysfunctional internal culture* — e.g., dishonesty, low employee morale and loyalty, lack of employee trust, and command-and-control tactics by upper management that inhibit employee flexibility and learning;

- *inferior competencies* — the core competencies required to sustain competitive advantage are not understood, or are inferior to competitor competencies;

- *absence of process advantage* — competitors have more efficient core business processes, resulting in the ability to maintain margins at more competitive prices;

- *ineffective internal communication* — e.g., managers hoard information and barriers exist that prevent the free and rapid flow of relevant information to those who need it.

Traditional risk management activities performed by organizations have focused on the local external operating environment. Some of the potentially significant business risks that can arise in this environment are:

- *direct competition* — direct competitors also adapt continually and improve their operations, and new competitors entering the market increase price competition;

- *local labor markets* — direct competitors compete for the best labor resources;

- *customer/supplier relationships* — e.g., an inferior customer service process;

- *competitor innovations* — new technologies that create process advantages for competitors.

As we approach the twenty-first century, forces emerging from outside of the local operating environment are bringing significant pressures to bear on the entity's profitability and survival. Some of these macroenvironmental forces, which might motivate the need for the entity to adapt its strategies, are:

- *lax regulatory environments in foreign countries* — competitors are producing the same products or product substitutes at lower costs;

- *natural resources* — a foreign competitor resides in a country rich in product raw material or direct competitors have stronger relationships with suppliers in these foreign countries;

- *global competition* — direct competition from new market entrants residing in foreign countries, or product innovations originating in other markets and industries that become direct product substitutes (for example, e-mail could force the U.S. Post Office to change its products, service, and production processes);

- *cultural advantages* — e.g., a strong work ethic and high degree of loyalty are part of the fabric of certain cultures.

Competitor strategic alliances and changes in the regulatory climate are additional discontinuous external forces that can impact an organization's ability to attain its business objectives and sustain its competitive advantage. Strategic alliances are symbiotic relationships that are being used with increasing frequency for several purposes, including establishing new niches and new barriers to market entry. Transparent connections between strategic partners, including suppliers and customers, create boundaryless organizations that are complex webs of interdependent business relationships. These webs can hinder access to customers and suppliers. Expanding regulations also are imposing additional burdens on organizations, and posing additional threats to the attainment of business objectives. Finally, in some industries, such as electric utilities, deregulation is thrusting organizations into new and unfamiliar business environments. Alliances and regulatory trends can be complex and can present unique challenges for the auditor as he attempts to develop an understanding of the alliance relationships and new regulations, their economic impacts, and their implications for management's accounting choices and disclosures.

In the sections that follow, we present KPMG's BMP knowledge acquisition framework — a framework that guides the auditor's collection and processing of information about the the client's strategies, supporting business processes, and the external forces that threaten the viability of its strategies. The BMP knowledge acquisition framework involves separate sub-analyses performed for each of the five components of the Beer viable-system hierarchy presented in an earlier section. The BMP client business model helps the auditor link and assimilate the data obtained from these sub-analyses into knowledge about the interactions among the five components, and between them and the organization's external environment.

6 A Proposed Knowledge Acquisition Framework for the Risk-Based Strategic-Systems Audit

[V]ariables that are actually coupled to the real system, influencing and being influenced by the rest of the system, must be modeled as endogenous variables embedded in information-feedback loops. Without that coupling, the model would fail to exhibit "modes of operation" that stem from the feedback effects the coupling generates. Some dynamic patterns would be missed or misrepresented.

Jay Forrester
Industrial Dynamics[32]

To effectively assess the client's ability to create value and generate cash flows, the auditor should develop a comprehensive understanding of the client's positioning within its value chain,[33] and its ability to create and sustain competitive advantage within that environment. A proposed framework[34] for obtaining that comprehensive understanding is presented below.

- *Understand the client's strategic advantage*: What is the client's plan for creating value? What are its niches and what are its advantages that make it better suited than its competitors to occupy these niches?

- *Understand the risks that threaten attainment of the client's business objectives*: What might prevent the client from creating targeted value? What forces are challenging its competitive advantages? How effective are its risk management, strategic management, and information management processes?

- *Understand the key processes and related competencies needed to realize strategic advantage*: What competencies and process advantages must the client possess to create targeted value? What are the business risks threatening attainment of its process objec-

---

32 Jay W. Forrester, *Industrial Dynamics* (MIT Press, Cambridge, MA, 1961), as paraphrased in George P. Richardson, *Feedback Thought in Social Science and Systems Theory* (University of Pennsylvania Press, Philadelphia, 1991), p. 153.
33 For seminal discussions of competitive positioning and value-chain analysis see M. E. Porter, *Competitive Strategy: Techniques for Analyzing Industries and Competitors* (The Free Press, New York, 1980); and M. E. Porter, *Competitive Advantage: Creating and Sustaining Superior Performance* (The Free Press, New York, 1985).
34 This framework is similar to the analytic strategy frame presented in C. W. Hofer and D. E. Schendel, *Strategy Formulation: Analytical Concepts* (West Publishing Co., St. Paul, MN,1978).

tives? Are its process objectives properly aligned with its strategic objectives? How effective are process controls at controlling process risks?

- *Measure and benchmark process performance*: Is there evidence that the expected value is actually being created? That is, how well are the processes actually performing, in terms of strategic goals, compared to the competition? How much above-normal profit is earned as a result of the realized strategic advantage and related process efficiencies?

- *Document the understanding of the client's ability to create value and generate future cash flows using a client business model, process analyses, key performance indicators, and a business risk profile*: Create a comprehensive business knowledge decision frame to serve as a strategic-systems lens through which professional judgments about management assertions can be made.

- *Use the comprehensive business knowledge decision frame to develop expectations about key assertions embodied in the overall financial statements.*

- *Compare reported financial results to expectations and design additional audit test work to address any gaps between expectations and reported results.*

Professional judgments about the proper recording of transactions, the appropriateness of assumptions underlying the accounting for nonroutine transactions and accounting estimates, the valuation of recorded assets, the client's ability to continue in existence, and the likelihood of management fraud should be grounded in a comprehensive understanding of the business — the way it creates value and the sustainability of its competitive advantage. In the absence of this comprehensive decision frame, there is no way of knowing when, and the extent to which, judgments are misguided.

7 The KPMG Business Measurement Process

There is, we have often insisted, no "right" or "correct" model of anything at all; there are only more or less appropriate models for particular purposes. If, however, we are to approach Plato's desideratum of discussing not some one particular aspect of an organized whole, but the whole of it at once, we need a model able to encompass not only the firm but all its interactions.

Stafford Beer

Decision and Control: The Meaning of Operational Research and Management Cybernetics[35]

Overview of BMP

The KPMG Business Measurement Process (BMP) has each of the features discussed in the preceding section. Under BMP, the auditor's work process is turned upside down, shifting the risk assessment focus from a transactions risk orientation to a strategic client business risk orientation.

BMP guides the focus, breadth, and depth of the auditor's knowledge acquisition, and supports his development of expectations about client operating results and financial condition. The methods and procedures comprising BMP are based on five principles of business monitoring and measurement: strategic analysis, business process analysis, risk assessment, business measurement, and continuous improvement. The five principles, and their interrelationships, are illustrated in Exhibit 4 [p. 34].[36]

Under BMP, risk assessment begins with a strategic analysis of the client. The BMP auditor analyzes the industry within which the client is operating, the client's strategy to achieve a sustainable competitive advantage within this industry context, the business risks that threaten the success of this strategy, and the client's responses to these risks.

---

35 Stafford Beer, *Decision and Control: The Meaning of Operational Research and Management Cybernetics* (John Wiley and Sons, London, 1966).
36 This type of model is similar to those proposed by R. Ackoff in his books *Concept of Corporate Planning* (John Wiley & Sons, New York, 1970) and *Redesigning the Future* (John Wiley & Sons, New York, 1980).

During strategic analysis,[37] the BMP auditor makes judgments about whether the client has advantages for occupying its current niches, whether external forces threaten the sustainability of these niches, and whether accounting choices are appropriate in light of the client's strategic positioning.

During the 1990s there has been a surge in activities involving the redesign of core business processes and the outsourcing of noncore processes as organizations attempt to achieve "process advantage."[38] Management traditionally has focused on business inputs and outputs, leaving the detailed operation of core business processes to lower-level operations personnel. Today, we see a shift toward process-driven competition, and thus, top management have turned their attention to creating process advantage. Similar to species in living nature, organizations that achieve process advantage are in a position to survive and prosper, whereas organizations stuck at lower levels of process performance risk extinction.

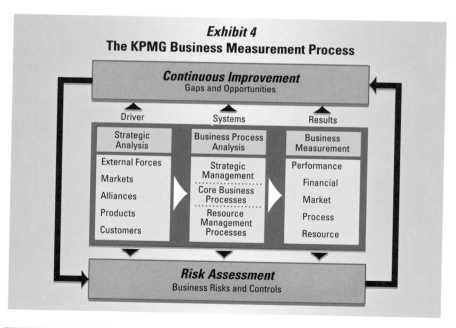

Exhibit 4
The KPMG Business Measurement Process

---

37 The methods and ideas that impacted the design of the BMP strategic analysis procedures include M. E. Porter's work, i.e., value-chain analysis and the five forces model, and the work of other leading thinkers in the fields of strategy and management.
38 See, for example, J. Champy and M. Hammer, *Reengineering the Corporation: A Manifesto for Business Revolution* (HarperBusiness, New York, 1993).

The BMP auditor analyzes key business processes of the client organization as a means of developing a broad understanding of the flow of activities comprising each process, how the processes interrelate with one another and with individuals and organizations outside of the entity, and those competencies and competitive advantages that determine the strengths of these interrelationships. During business process analysis, the BMP auditor identifies significant process risks and comes to understand how they are being controlled. Measurements of process performance are taken by the BMP auditor to identify performance gaps between client processes and analogous processes of direct competitors demonstrating consistent process advantage. Also, the BMP auditor gains an understanding of critical key performance measures used to manage performance of the organization's key business processes, and considers the extent to which these measures can be used as corroborating evidence to support his expectations about financial-statement assertions.

The BMP auditor gains an understanding of the client's own risk management processes and the extent to which the client is monitoring external and internal risks[39] that threaten the achievement of its overall business objectives and its business-process objectives. The primary goal of management control is to ensure that risk monitoring and control activities are aligned properly with overall strategic objectives. An adequate risk management process will include sub-processes at the strategic level and the business-process level, with an effective management control process to integrate and coordinate the monitoring and control activities occurring at both levels. Strategic business risks threaten the overall success of the entity's business strategy, i.e., the strengths of its connections with its environment, while process business risks threaten the achievement of specific process objectives.

Once the auditor gains an understanding of management's process for identifying and controlling business risks, and management's perceptions, assumptions, and judgments about business risks, he can assess the business risk implications, both for the client's business and for the audit approach. Particular attention is paid to the adequacy of the risk management process, and includes considerations such as whether these business risks identified by management are complete; business risks have been prioritized appropriately; existing controls reduce these risks to acceptable levels; and accounting choices and financial disclosures properly reflect uncontrolled risks.

---

39 External risks, including operational, financial, and compliance risks, arise from the complex relationships between the organization and elements of its external environment. Internal risks arise from characteristics of, and interactions among, the organization's management, strategy, structure, culture, and business processes.

During the business measurement phase of the BMP audit, the auditor measures the processes and variables that have the greatest impact on the business. He also analyzes interrelated performance measures (financial and nonfinancial) both over time and relative to those of similar organizations. Transactions-based auditing procedures, framed by using the comprehensive client business model to support the development of expectations through the broader strategic-systems lens, are applied to non-routine transactions and non-routine and highly judgmental accounting estimates. Computer-assisted auditing techniques also might be applied to populations of routine transactions to filter those that are unusual in nature.[40] Additional audit test work is performed when interrelated financial and nonfinancial performance measures are inconsistent, and when key financial-statement assertions are not consistent with the auditor's understanding of the organization's strategic-systems dynamics, including its strategy and measures of process performance.

The development of a comprehensive client business model positions the BMP auditor to provide valuable feedback from an independent monitor, not just to outside capital suppliers, but also to inside process owners, board members, and top management. During the continuous improvement phase of the audit, the auditor prepares and reports process performance and financial performance gap analyses using standardized target measures, and measures from competitors that have demonstrated consistent process advantage. In addition, the auditor identifies and reports on the process areas that, if improved, could achieve the "process advantages" the client seeks. These new types of diagnostic business assurance are natural by-products of the BMP audit that provide additional benefits to client organizations.

A detailed discussion of the monitoring and measurement principles upon which the BMP approach is based is presented next.

BMP — Detailed Discussion with Illustrations

Similar to a traditional auditor, the BMP auditor is concerned about assessing the three components of audit risk — inherent, control, and detection risks. The BMP auditor, however, grounds his judgments in a much broader view of the client than does an auditor following a transactions-detail audit approach. He uses more holistic perspectives to frame the assessment of the validity of the financial statements taken as a whole, and the account balances contained therein.

---

[40] Transactions that fail to pass through screening filters are subjected to further testing. Client analyses and internal audit results are relied upon when appropriate.

As discussed in the prior section, the BMP framework comprises five principles that guide the auditor's monitoring and measurement of a client's key business activities: (1) strategic analysis, (2) business process analysis, (3) risk assessment, (4) business measurement, and (5) continuous improvement. Analytical procedures embodying each principle are both grounded in a broad and rich understanding of the client organization's environment, and provide the vehicle by which such an understanding is acquired. These procedures have been designed to help the BMP auditor answer the following key questions about the client's strategy, organizational design, and strategic-systems dynamics:

- Do the client's strategy and the business relationships it has formed address the external forces in the industry?

- Does the design of the business processes established by the client support its strategic objectives?

- Has management gained a complete perception of the business risks that could affect achievement of the strategic and business-process objectives?

- Are management's assumptions about the significance of those risks reasonable?

- Does the design of the control framework established by the client adequately address identified risks?

- Does management monitor and measure those factors that are critical to the achievement of its business objectives and the management of its significant business risks?

The BMP Business Model

The BMP auditor uses a "client business model" to organize and integrate the information he gathers about the client's business and industry. The business model is a tool that helps the auditor develop an understanding of the effectiveness of the design and management of the client's business, and of the critical performance-related issues it faces, to better evaluate audit risk. When completed, the client business model is a strategic-systems decision frame that describes the interlinking activities carried out within a business entity, the external forces that bear upon the entity, and the business relationships with persons and other organizations outside of the entity. The client business model framework is presented in Exhibit 5 [p. 38].

The eight components comprising the client business model are:

- *External Forces* — political, economic, social, and technological factors, pressures, and forces from outside the entity that threaten the attainment of the entity's business objectives;

- *Markets/Formats* — the domains in which the entity may choose to operate, and the design and location of the facilities;

- *Strategic Management Process* — the process by which the:
  - entity's mission is developed
  - entity's business objectives are defined
  - business risks that threaten attainment of the business objecttives are identified
  - business risk management processes are established
  - progress toward meeting business objectives is monitored;

- *Core Business Processes* — the processes that develop, produce, market, and distribute an entity's products and services. These processes do not necessarily follow traditional organizational or functional lines, but reflect the interlinkage of related business activities;

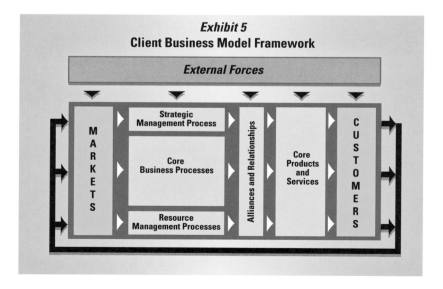

Exhibit 5
Client Business Model Framework

- *Resource Management Processes* — the processes by which resources are acquired, developed, and allocated to the core business activities;

- *Alliances* — the relationships established by an entity to:
  - attain business objectives
  - expand business opportunities
  - reduce or transfer business risk;

- *Core Products and Services* — the commodities that the entity brings to the market; and

- *Customers* — the individuals and organizations that purchase the entity's output.

Again, use of the client business model to organize and integrate client business and industry information helps ensure that the BMP auditor gives the proper degree of consideration to significant client business risks and their possible impacts on audit risk. The business measurement and monitoring principles and related analytical procedures represent the activities that the BMP auditor performs to acquire knowledge about the client's business and industry for the purpose of completing the full client business model template. Throughout his performance of these analytical procedures, the BMP auditor is working toward the ultimate goal of integrating the knowledge he obtains about the five hierarchical components of a viable system (discussed in an earlier section) to gain insights about the client's systems dynamics and the congruence between strategy and the environment. He may use mental processes or more formal business simulation and systems thinking tools, or some combination of both, to structure his thinking about the client's strategic-systems dynamics. The processes the BMP auditor uses to mentally assimilate the acquired knowledge will be unique for each client and for each auditor, and therefore cannot, and should not, be reduced to highly structured formats, such as templates, checklists, or mathematical models.

BMP Strategic Analysis

The strategic-systems lens focuses the auditor's attention on whether managers have designed effective strategies for reshaping patterns of behavior. The BMP strategic analysis is intended to provide the auditor with a deep understanding of the broad environment in which the client organization operates, and focuses on the organization's strategic orientation and potential for reorientation.[41] Included therein are both the industry and global environs of the client organization. Also included is the BMP auditor's understanding of the client's strategy for achieving a sustainable competitive advantage within the industry context. Consistently, the business risks that threaten achievement of this strategy are identified along with the client's responses to such risks.

As part of the strategic analysis, the BMP auditor will obtain or update an understanding of the client organization's history, its management's business strategy and objectives, the business risks faced by the client organization, management's planned responses to such business risks, and the business processes that management have implemented. The strategic analysis also is focused on the articulation between the business strategy and the supporting business processes as well as the articulation between the identified business risks and management's responses.

During strategic analysis, the BMP auditor may first obtain general industry information, including that which is available from trade associations, periodicals, etc. Then, he will consider obtaining information about the structure of the industry, including its segmentation, the dynamics among the various organizations that comprise the industry, the critical business issues facing entities in the industry, and significant industry risks. KPMG has developed (and updates as reasonably practicable) Industry Segment Business Models, which contain the aforementioned information.

Exhibit 6 presents a general BMP Segment Business Model for the Retail line of business. As shown in Exhibit 6, possible external forces for this industry segment include lifestyle trends, new entrants, regulation, technology, and suppliers. Thus, if the client organization were a restaurant chain, the BMP auditor would be cognizant of the trend toward two-income families, which, in turn, creates a propensity for eating in restaurants and purchasing prepared food in grocery stores. For the Retail line of business, potential markets include stores (e.g., department, specialty, restaurants, drug, grocery, convenience, outlet) and non-stores (e.g., catalogue, electronic home shopping, direct mail). Customers for the Retail line of business include individuals (differentiated on a variety of demographics including age, gender, income, and education), resellers, not-for-profit institutions, government, and commercial entities. Alliances and other relationship possibilities include joint ventures, vendor partnering, and trade associations.

---

41 See P. Gorman, M. Pruett, and H. Thomas, "Development of Competitive Strategies," *Concise International Encyclopedia of Business and Management*, Malcolm Warner, ed. (Routledge, London & New York, 1996), pp. 692 - 710.

Core products and services in this line of business include soft goods, hard goods (durable and nondurable), food, and various support services, including credit extension, delivery and installation, repair, service contracts, etc. From a "value chain" perspective, core business processes for the Retail line of business are Brand and Image Delivery, Product/Service Delivery, and Customer Service Delivery. Resource management processes for this line of business include human resource management, property management, regulatory management, financial/treasury management, and information management.

The BMP auditor constructs the eight-component business model for the client and its environment by tailoring the general Industry Segment Business Model to reflect the client's specific niche(s) and idiosyncrasies. Client businesses are complex and diverse and so the Segment Business

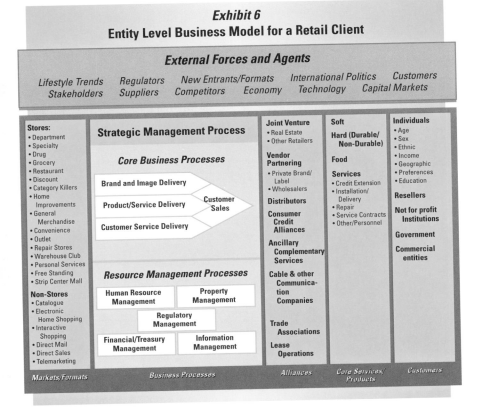

Exhibit 6
Entity Level Business Model for a Retail Client

Model serves only as a starting point for understanding the client. It is certain that the general Industry Segment Business Model will not reflect all of the client's idiosyncrasies, and that differences will matter.

At the conclusion of the strategic analysis, the BMP auditor will have learned the "directional course" the client has set in response to the environment, taking into consideration:

- the relationship between the broad economic environment and the industry segment(s) in which the client competes;

- the client's position and role within its respective industry segment(s);

- threats to the client's current position;

- the needs and wants of the client's chosen market segment(s);

- the total productive capacity of the client and its competitors for each niche;

- management's vision of how to better satisfy the market needs than its rivals; and

- management's specific strategies and plans for achieving that vision.

Also, the auditor will have obtained an understanding of how the client "steers" the business, and attains a "fit" between its strategy and the range of environmental forces, through his review of the:

- client's strategic management process;

- formalized strategic plan;

- client's approach to "environmental scanning" to monitor emerging or changing external threats;

- client's methods for communicating strategies throughout the organization, and the clarity of such communications; and

- client's methods and measures used to monitor entity-level performance in terms of its strategic goals.

And, most importantly, the BMP auditor will have considered the audit implications of the client's strategy and strategic management process by addressing questions like:

- What are the implications of the client's business strategy and strategic business risks for underlying accounting choices and financial-statement disclosures?

- Do accounting estimates and valuations reflect significant business risks?
- How will the client's strategic risks impact additional audit work at the business process or transactions levels?

BMP Business Process Analysis

The BMP Business Process Analysis is designed to provide the auditor with an in-depth understanding of the key business processes identified earlier in the audit. Via this analysis, the BMP auditor learns how the client organization creates value. Specifically, each key core business process[42] is studied in depth to discern significant process objectives, the business risks related to these objectives, the controls established to mitigate the risks, and the financial-statement implications of the risks and controls. Consistently, each significant resource management process is examined with the same foci. During the business process analysis, the BMP auditor also will identify classes of transactions that appear to pose differential misstatement risks (e.g., routine versus non-routine transactions and accounting estimates) as well as the associated financial-statement account balances.

Business process analysis adopts a "value chain"[43] approach to analyzing the interconnected activities in the client's business, both domestically and globally. It is consistent with W. Edward Deming's views of business processes and the role of total quality management in monitoring the value of these processes. Core business processes represent the main customer-facing activities of the business. It is the successful combination and execution of the core business processes that create value in the eyes of customers and, therefore, result in profitable customer sales. During business process analysis, the BMP auditor recognizes the cross-functional nature of activities in the client's business. Also, he recognizes that not all activities within and across processes are sequential, and that important linkages exist between processes.

Exhibit 7 [p. 44] presents the process analysis template used by the BMP auditor to analyze the client's core business processes and significant resource management processes. The template is a framework that guides

---

42 The BMP auditor identifies the key business processes that will be analyzed in-depth based on his understanding of the business strategy, and the competencies required to successfully carry out that strategy.
43 See M. E. Porter, *Competitive Advantage: Creating and Sustaining Superior Performance* (The Free Press, New York, 1985) for an in-depth discussion of value chain analysis.

the BMP auditor's collection and integration of information about business processes using eight dimensions: process objectives, inputs, activities, outputs, systems, classes of transactions, risks that threaten objectives, and other symptoms of poor performance. Refer to Exhibit 7 for descriptions of each of these dimensions.

Returning to the Retail line of business, its core business processes are Brand and Image Delivery, Product/Service Delivery and Customer Service Delivery. Exhibit 8 presents the typical sub-processes found in these three core business processes.

Consider, for example, the Brand and Image Delivery core business process, which includes the following sub-processes: format development and site selection, brand management, advertising and promotion, visual merchandising, and proprietary credit. Exhibit 9 [p. 46] presents an example of a

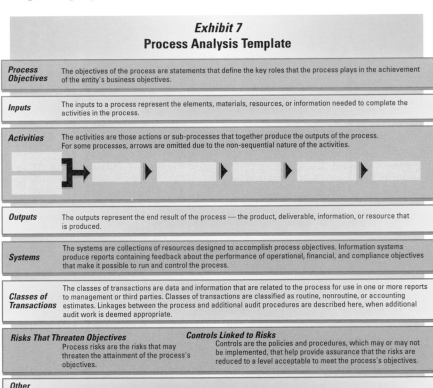

Exhibit 7
Process Analysis Template

Process Objectives
The objectives of the process are statements that define the key roles that the process plays in the achievement of the entity's business objectives.

Inputs
The inputs to a process represent the elements, materials, resources, or information needed to complete the activities in the process.

Activities
The activities are those actions or sub-processes that together produce the outputs of the process. For some processes, arrows are omitted due to the non-sequential nature of the activities.

Outputs
The outputs represent the end result of the process — the product, deliverable, information, or resource that is produced.

Systems
The systems are collections of resources designed to accomplish process objectives. Information systems produce reports containing feedback about the performance of operational, financial, and compliance objectives that make it possible to run and control the process.

Classes of Transactions
The classes of transactions are data and information that are related to the process for use in one or more reports to management or third parties. Classes of transactions are classified as routine, nonroutine, or accounting estimates. Linkages between the process and additional audit procedures are described here, when additional audit work is deemed appropriate.

Risks That Threaten Objectives
Process risks are the risks that may threaten the attainment of the process's objectives.

Controls Linked to Risks
Controls are the policies and procedures, which may or may not be implemented, that help provide assurance that the risks are reduced to a level acceptable to meet the process's objectives.

Other Symptoms of Poor Performance
Other symptoms of poor performance comprise other evidence that indicates the process may not be operating to its most effective level.

completed process analysis template for the format and site selection sub-process. The BMP auditor would address each of the following objectives, which are typical for this process: (1) provide an environment in which the customer's needs can be met; (2) deliver a cost-effective and viable shop solution; (3) inject freshness and maintain a competitive edge; (4) use the store as a vehicle for differentiation; (5) open the store on time and stay on budget; and (6) take maximum advantage of available financial incentives. From a value-chain perspective, and focusing first on inputs, historical performance, technology capability, competitor formats, customer profile, and cost constraints are among the key considerations.

Continuing the value-chain perspective, the BMP auditor will gather information about activities such as review and selection of format options, store design, store mock-up and research, developer and contract selection, etc. And, the BMP auditor will consider outputs like the following: (1) store design; (2) the macro-space plan; (3) recruitment and training; (4) customer satisfaction measures, and (5) the roll-out implementation plan.

The BMP auditor also will recognize that various client systems are germane to the brand and image delivery sub-process of format development and site selection. These systems include the customer database, space management, property development and construction, market research, project appraisal, and contract management systems. The BMP auditor further will identify transactions of relevance using the aforementioned trichotomy: (1) *routine transactions* — store pre-opening costs, depreciation, merchandise purchases, and fixture purchases; *nonroutine transactions* — design agency and construction contracts, landlord/developer contributions; and *accounting estimates* — provision for obsolete fixtures.

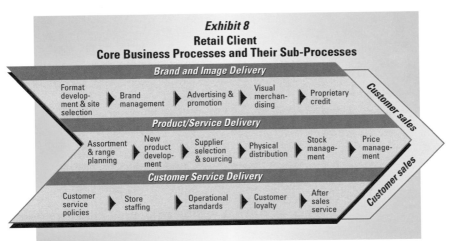

Exhibit 8
Retail Client
Core Business Processes and Their Sub-Processes

Exhibit 9
Retail Client
Core Business Process: Brand and Image Delivery
Sub Process: Format Development and Site Selection

Process Objectives		
• Provide shopping environment that meets customer needs	• Provide a source of differentiation	
• Deliver a cost-effective and viable shop solution	• Open store on time and on budget	
• Inject freshness and maintain a competitive edge	• Take maximum advantage of available financial incentives	

Inputs		
• Historical performance	• Customer profile	• Customer research (format specific)
• Technology capability	• Location planning	• Supply chain/stock process
• Review of competitor formats	• Operating standards and constraints	• Cost constraints
• Political, legal and environmental influences	• Transport facilities	• Fixturing sources
• Rent or buy implications	• Landlord	• Return on investment target
• Merchandise plan	• Format lifestage	

Activities

Review and selection of format options	▶	Brief store design	▶	Construct mock up and test/research	▶	Qualify and select developers and contractors	▶	Develop pilot program and trial store operations	▶	Monitor and evaluate	▶	Manage construction and build out	▶	Perform new store/remodel opening

Outputs		
• Store design	• Customer satisfaction measure	• Capital expenditure budget
• Macro space plan	• Roll out implementation plan	• Marketing plan
• Pilot/control store framework	• Information technology requirements	• New property
• Recruitment and training	• Cost/revenue appraisal	• New leases

Systems		
• Customer database	• Market research systems	• Geographic information systems
• Space management systems	• Project appraisal systems	• Contract management system
• Property development and construction system		

Classes of Transactions	*Routine*	*Non-Routine*	*Accounting Estimates*
	• Store pre-opening costs	• Design agency and construction contracts	• Provision for obsolete fixtures
	• Depreciation	• Landlord/developer contribution	
	• Merchandise purchases		
	• Fixture purchases		

Risks That Threaten Objectives	**Controls Linked to Risks**
• Lack of adequate market and customer research leading evaluation to overestimate potential new format performance	• Formal market and customer research process, including post-launch
• Competitors develop better formats	• Regular competitor monitoring and contingency planning
• Cost overruns (pilot and roll out)	• Capital expenditure approval procedures
• Too much focus on new stores leading to neglect of comparable stores performance	• Project management procedures
• Select appropriate design agency	• Evaluation criteria and control
• Missed financial incentives	• Design agency screening and selection procedure
	• Appropriate experts

Other Symptoms of Poor Performance		
• Cannibalization of sales from existing stores	• Poor operational standards and execution	• Low customer awareness/satisfaction of new format
• Missed deadlines		

The BMP auditor next considers the risks that threaten achievement of the process objectives, and the controls that have been implemented to mitigate such risks. Continuing with the focus on the format and site selection sub-process, such risks may include the possibility that competitors will develop better store formats, and an overemphasis on new stores relative to existing stores. Controls that could mitigate such risks are regular monitoring of competitors in concert with contingency planning and usage of appropriate evaluation criteria.

A similar approach is taken by the BMP auditor for the significant resource management processes, which earlier were identified to be financial/treasury management, information management, human resource management, property management, and regulatory management. Exhibit 10 [p. 48] presents an example of a completed process analysis template for a retail client's human resource management process. As shown in Exhibit 10, the following are among the process objectives of relevance: attract and retain a skilled and motivated work force; control employee costs while maintaining morale and productivity; comply with regulatory/tax filing requirements; and adhere to the organization's code of conduct. Maintaining a value-chain perspective, the BMP auditor next considers inputs to this process including the organization's strategic plan, its operating plan, employee regulations, tax regulations, union contracts, industry statistics and market data, and training goals. Activities such as developing and maintaining human resource policies and procedures, establishing and maintaining compensation and benefit policies and programs, identifying resource requirements, recruitment and hiring, training and development, performance reviews, compensation and benefit administration, monitoring of union contracts and grievances, and monitoring compliance with regulations are then considered.

The BMP auditor then will consider outputs such as regulatory filings, personnel files, tax filings, performance reviews, etc. Of course, various systems will be recognized as keys to successful human resource management. These systems include those for compensation and benefits, tax compliance, and regulatory compliance. Again, key transaction classes are noted using the trichotomy: (1) *routine* — payroll and benefit taxes, payroll accruals, and training expenses; (2) *non-routine* — pensions, other post-retirement benefits, post-employment benefits, and incentive compensation accruals; and (3) *accounting estimates* — self-insured medical costs, self-insured workers' compensation, and self-insured general liability claims.

Subsequently, the BMP auditor considers risks related to the human resource management function, including high levels of staff turnover, non-compliance with regulations, and noncompetitive compensation packages. In turn, the auditor considers the controls that can mitigate such risks. For the risks just identified, these controls would include implementing growth and opportunity plans for employees, regulatory monitoring, and benchmarking salary costs against industry and other norms.

At the conclusion of business process analysis, the BMP auditor will have updated his understanding of a) how the client creates value, b) whether the

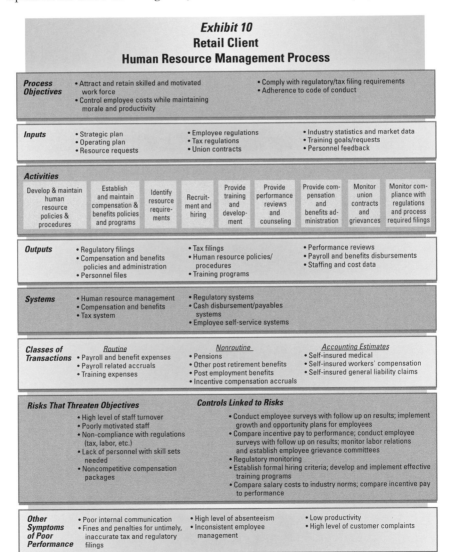

Exhibit 10
Retail Client
Human Resource Management Process

Process Objectives
- Attract and retain skilled and motivated work force
- Control employee costs while maintaining morale and productivity
- Comply with regulatory/tax filing requirements
- Adherence to code of conduct

Inputs
- Strategic plan
- Operating plan
- Resource requests
- Employee regulations
- Tax regulations
- Union contracts
- Industry statistics and market data
- Training goals/requests
- Personnel feedback

Activities

Develop & maintain human resource policies & procedures	Establish and maintain compensation & benefits policies and programs	Identify resource requirements	Recruitment and hiring	Provide training and development	Provide performance reviews and counseling	Provide compensation and benefits administration	Monitor union contracts and grievances	Monitor compliance with regulations and process required filings

Outputs
- Regulatory filings
- Compensation and benefits policies and administration
- Personnel files
- Tax filings
- Human resource policies/procedures
- Training programs
- Performance reviews
- Payroll and benefits disbursements
- Staffing and cost data

Systems
- Human resource management
- Compensation and benefits
- Tax system
- Regulatory systems
- Cash disbursement/payables systems
- Employee self-service systems

Classes of Transactions

Routine	Nonroutine	Accounting Estimates
• Payroll and benefit expenses	• Pensions	• Self-insured medical
• Payroll related accruals	• Other post retirement benefits	• Self-insured workers' compensation
• Training expenses	• Post employment benefits	• Self-insured general liability claims
	• Incentive compensation accruals	

Risks That Threaten Objectives
- High level of staff turnover
- Poorly motivated staff
- Non-compliance with regulations (tax, labor, etc.)
- Lack of personnel with skill sets needed
- Noncompetitive compensation packages

Controls Linked to Risks
- Conduct employee surveys with follow up on results; implement growth and opportunity plans for employees
- Compare incentive pay to performance; conduct employee surveys with follow up on results; monitor labor relations and establish employee grievance committees
- Regulatory monitoring
- Establish formal hiring criteria; develop and implement effective training programs
- Compare salary costs to industry norms; compare incentive pay to performance

Other Symptoms of Poor Performance
- Poor internal communication
- Fines and penalties for untimely, inaccurate tax and regulatory filings
- High level of absenteeism
- Inconsistent employee management
- Low productivity
- High level of customer complaints

client has aligned effectively the business process activities with the business strategy, c) what are the significant process risks that threaten the achievement of the client's business objectives, and d) how effective the processes are at controlling the significant strategic and process risks to identify the financial-statement audit implications of business process activities and the attendant business risks and controls. This detailed and updated knowledge about the client's business provides a basis for the auditor's development of expectations about its operating results and financial condition.

BMP Risk Assessment

Risk assessment is a continuous process performed throughout the BMP audit. During strategic analysis and business process analysis, the auditor reviews the processes and procedures that the client has established to identify and manage strategic and process risks. Before describing some of the activities the BMP auditor performs during these process reviews and during risk assessment, we provide a brief overview of the new business risk control paradigm that is changing the way organizations manage their business risks.

The New Business Risk Control Paradigm

Businesses have, over the years, used a variety of practices to control risk. In many organizations, however, control is a misunderstood and misapplied concept. In these instances, control all too often means inflexible and unimaginative budgets, seemingly endless management reporting requirements, and an over-burdening and often irrelevant stream of information up and down the corporate hierarchy.

Fast-moving markets, flattening corporate hierarchies, and the need for an expanding scope of authority at the local level are making salient the costs of misunderstanding and misapplying control. In response, managers are rethinking fundamental definitions of control, and how business risks should be identified and mitigated.

Clearly, a major business risk is management's preparation and distribution of misleading financial statements and other information to investors, creditors, and employees. Organizations, therefore, will continue to invest significant resources to guard against such risk. And the auditor's professional risk will continue to be reduced by developing an understanding of the implications of business risk on the financial statements and related disclosures. The approaches to and mechanisms by which control is achieved, however, as illustrated in Exhibit 11 [p. 50], will be different.

Because auditors are recognized for their knowledge of controls, they are in a unique position to influence control policy as it evolves in organizations recognizing the control paradigm shift. More importantly, however, auditors' thinking about control must evolve — e.g., empowerment will increasingly blur lines of authority and increasingly flat organizations will provide fewer opportunities for segregation of duties. Auditors' traditional notions of control as segregation of duties and functions, proper authorization for expenditures, controlled access to assets, proper recording of transactions, etc., that "define the procedural checks and balances that safeguard assets and assure integrity of data"[44] must be recognized as only one aspect of the contemporary organization's control mosaic.

Other components of the control mosaic include diagnostic control systems, belief systems, boundary systems, and incentives. Diagnostic control systems, for example, recognize that empowerment requires a change in

Exhibit 11
Comparison of Traditional and New Business Risk Control Paradigms

Old Paradigm	*New Paradigm*
Risk assessment occurs periodically	Risk assessment is a continuous process
Accounting, treasury, and internal audit responsible for identifying risks and managing controls	Business risk identification and control management are the responsibility of all members of the organization
Fragmentation—every function behaves independently	Connection—Business risk assessment and control are focused and coordinated with senior-level oversight
Control is focused on financial risk avoidance	Control is focused on the avoidance of unacceptable business risk, followed closely by management of other unavoidable business risks to reduce them to an acceptable level
Business risk controls policies, if established, generally do not have the full support of upper management or are inadequately communicated throughout the company	A formal business risk controls policy is approved by management and board and communicated throughout the company
Inspect and detect business risk, then react at the source	Anticipate and prevent business risk, and monitor business risk controls continuously
Ineffective people are the primary source of business risk	Ineffective processes are the primary source of business risk

44 Robert Simms, *Levels of Control* (Harvard Business School Press, 1995), p. 196.

what is controlled. Traditionally, inputs and processes have been controlled. Absent such controls, however, empowered subordinates are made accountable for performance and diagnostic control systems measure and monitor such performance. Consistently, empowered individuals effectively are asked to take risks and there must be commensurate rewards for such risk taking and achievement of superior performance. Such rewards, which either can be monetary or nonmonetary (e.g., public praise and recognition), are made on the basis of tangible performance consistent with the organization's mission.

The evolving organizational controls structure consists of strategic control processes, management control processes, and business process control processes. A brief description of these elements follows:

- *Strategic control* — These processes are designed to continuously assess the effect of changes in environment risks on the business, formulate business risk control strategies, and align the organization with those strategies.

- *Management control* — These processes drive business risk assessment and control throughout the organization.

- *Process control* — These processes are designed to continuously assess the risks that business processes do not achieve what they were designed to achieve. Embedded in process risk is information processing/technology risk, which occurs when the information technologies used in the process are not operating as intended or are compromising the availability, security, integrity, relevance, and credibility of information produced.

BMP Risk Assessment Activities

During his reviews of the client's risk management processes, the BMP auditor develops an understanding of management's perceptions of business risk, both strategic business risks and business process business risks, and considers the reasonableness of the assumptions that underlie management's assessments of the potential impacts of these risks. These underlying assumptions may be viewed as a combination of assumptions about the probability of occurrence and assumptions about the magnitude of impact. Also, the BMP auditor uses other information obtained during the strategic and business process analyses to make judgments about coverage, i.e., whether management has considered all significant business risks. And he uses this information to make judgments about the extent to which strategic and process risks remain uncontrolled, i.e., to determine the level of residual risk.

Next, the BMP auditor further integrates information about residual business risks by grouping risks based on the particular financial-statement assertions to which they relate. Also, he will consider possible interactions among these groups of risks, and develop expectations about how they might be manifested in the financial statements. This integrated knowledge, together with the business measurements discussed in the next section, provide the BMP auditor with a basis for performing a diagnosis of the assertions embodied in the financial statements, and guides his tactical planning about the type and extent of additional evidence he should obtain to form an opinion about the validity of the assertions.

At the conclusion of the audit, the BMP auditor will have developed a business risk profile of the client organization. In the business risk profile, residual business risks are classified as either strategic or process risks. Also, interactions among risks are identified in the business risk profile, and the risk classifications and identified interactions are cross-matched with related financial-statement assertions. The BMP auditor will use the business risk profile to assist his final review of the adjusted financial statements.

BMP Business Measurement

Similar to BMP risk assessment, business measurement is performed on an ongoing basis during a BMP audit. The BMP auditor measures the business processes and variables which appear to have the greatest impact on the client organization, and analyzes interrelated key performance measures (financial and nonfinancial) over time and relative to similar organizations. Also, the BMP auditor assesses the client's revenue recognition practices, and the quality of the client's reported earnings, in terms of their impact on the validity of the related financial-statement assertions. These measurements and assessments are combined with the BMP auditor's knowledge about residual business risks and documented in the client business model.

The updated client business model, and the mental or more formal simulations performed by the auditor to better understand the client's strategic-systems dynamics, provide an evidential base for development of expectations about the entity's achieved level of overall performance, and about assertions embodied in specific account balances and classes of transactions. And, when his expectations and management's financial-statement assertions are significantly different, the updated client business model arms the BMP auditor with the kind of information he needs to diagnose symptoms and develop and test related hypotheses about the causes of the unexpected deviations.

To assess the quality of earnings (and in some cases the quality of other relevant performance measures), the BMP auditor considers three dimensions: (1) the accuracy of reported earnings — more conservative accounting practices generally will produce higher-quality earnings; (2) the overall permanence of earnings — the ability to sustain the current level of reported earnings in future periods; and (3) the correlation between the client's reported earnings and cash flows — the stronger the correlation between a client's earnings and cash flows, the higher the quality of earnings. These dimensions, in turn, relate to one or more of the following: stability of income-statement components, recoverability of assets, and capital maintenance.

One approach taken by the BMP auditor is to analyze the client's accounting practices and compare them against common industry practices. Such comparison will highlight practices that differ from the industry norm and may be suggestive of heightened risk. Possible earnings management practices that are not necessarily inappropriate, but suggestive of heightened risk, include: *Impression Management* — influencing the perceptions of others via choices based on the ability to report short-term as opposed to long-term income; *Income Smoothing* — management of the reported growth of earnings; and *Other Earnings Management Activities* — e.g., engaging in and structuring activities (e.g., financing) around their accounting income effect rather than for other business purposes. Examples of the types of cues that the BMP auditor would seek are presented in Exhibit 12 [p. 54].

During business measurement, the BMP auditor also evaluates the performance of the entity taken as a whole, and its key business processes, using key performance indicators (KPIs) and the collective knowledge contained in the client business model. KPIs are quantitative measurements, both financial and non-financial, collected by an entity or by the BMP auditor, either continuously or periodically, and used by management and the auditor to evaluate performance in terms of the entity's defined business objectives. KPIs at the process level focus on three dimensions of process performance: cycle time, process quality, and process costs. More specifically, management might monitor and control process performance using one or more of the following types of KPIs:

- waste, rework, and other indicators of process inefficiency;
- backlog of work in process;

- customer response time;
- number of times work is recycled between sub-processes and departments;
- number of document errors;
- customer satisfaction ratings;
- number of routing errors;
- value-adding processing time; and
- information processing errors.

KPIs that are not biased by financial-statement assertions, and that are obtained from reliable sources, can provide evidence to support the auditor's opinion. KPIs can provide evidence that business risks addressed by specific business processes are being controlled effectively, and they can be used as substantive tests to obtain evidential matter about particular assertions at the account balance or class of transactions level. For example, for a Retail client, a KPI measuring "order fulfillment cycle time" might provide evidence that business risk related to the order fulfillment process (e.g., customer dissatisfaction that could result in a significant decline in sales) is being controlled effectively. Of course, in this case the auditor's confidence about the quality of earnings also would be heightened. In addition, this key performance indicator could assist the BMP auditor's development of expectations about

Exhibit 12
Earnings Quality Indicators

Factor	Indicators of Higher Quality Earnings	Indicators of Lower Quality Earnings
Accruals and other accounting estimates	Consistent year-to-year	Frequently altered as pre-accrual income fluctuates
Accounting changes	Decrease income and seldom occur	Increase income and frequently occur
Income recognition	Reflects underlying cash flows	Occurs long in advance of cash flows
Disclosure level	High	Low

ending inventory, total sales for the period, cost of goods sold, and whether the accounting recognition of year-end sales has been cut off appropriately.

In Exhibit 13 [p. 56], we use a causal loop diagram[45] to depict the linkage between KPIs and financial-statement assertions. For the purpose of illustration, assume that the subject client is a mail-order computer manufacturing and retailing company whose current market niche is customers who are technically-knowledgeable users. Recent sales growth has imposed additional stress on the company's customer service process, and this stress coupled with intensifying competition in the company's market niche has caused management concern about the ability to maintain profit margins in the long run. Further, assume that management has decided to reorient its strategy and plans to use funds from growth to increase the quality of its customer support service to maintain its profit margin. Concurrently, management plans to expand to overseas markets, and expand its domestic market by broadening its corporate customer base.

In Exhibit 13, the loop labeled R1 (R signifies a reinforcing, or self-amplifying, behavioral dynamic) illustrates that increasing demand for the company's product feeds expansion, which feeds back to further increase demand. The signs presented in the diagram indicate the direction of the impact of the incoming feedback/action on the linked feedback/response. A positive sign indicates a reinforcing, or amplifying, impact and a negative sign indicates a dampening, or balancing, impact. For example, in loop R1, increasing demand generates increasing revenue, and increasing revenue provides additional funds for expansion into new markets. Expansion, in turn, leads to a further increase in demand. In the absence of balancing forces, we would expect that successive turns through the reinforcing feedback loop would grow sales revenue in perpetuity.

The loop labeled B2 (B signifies a balancing, or dampening, influence)[46] shows that increasing demand for the company's product will lead to a reduction in technical support quality if technical support capacity remains

---

45 A causal loop diagram is a systems analysis tool that can be used to develop a visual representation of the structure of a dynamic system. It contains one or more feedback loops that are either reinforcing or balancing that depict cause-and-effect relationships embedded in the system. For more information on feedback loops, see George P. Richardson, *Feedback Thought in Social Science and Systems Theory* (University of Pennsylvania Press, Philadelphia, 1991). The example presented here was adapted from V. Anderson and L. Johnson, *Systems Thinking Basics: From Concepts to Causal Loops* (Pegasus Communications, Inc., Cambridge, MA, 1997).
46 The direction of the influence of any individual loop can be determined by counting the number of negative links (signs) in it. A loop will be a balancing, or negative, loop whenever it contains an odd number of negative links, just as the product of an array of signed numbers will be negative when the array contains an odd quantity of negative numbers.

constant. Given the positive relationship between technical support quality and product demand, decreasing technical support quality will lead ultimately to a reduction in product demand, which, in turn will lead to an ultimate increase, or rebound, in technical support quality.[47]

The counterbalancing dynamic depicted by loop B2 will motivate management to expand technical support capacity, which can further complicate the client's systems dynamics. For example, loop B3 shows that a reduction in technical support quality increases the quality gap, which prompts an investment in capacity. Adding capacity eventually improves technical support

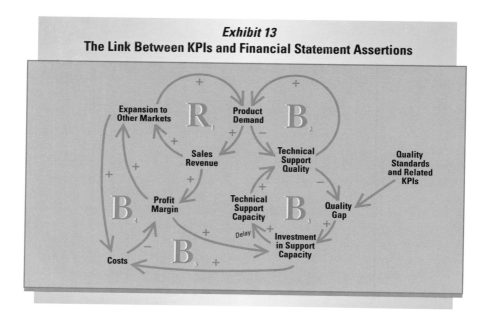

Exhibit 13
The Link Between KPIs and Financial Statement Assertions

---

[47] Balancing, or negative, feedback loops are believed to be a source of the dynamic of "oscillation" exhibited by many systems. Consider James Watt's centrifugal governor for the steam engine, which is a negative feedback loop. In its attempt to maintain a constant speed, the steam governor will cause an oscillation of the actual speed around its set point, the desired speed. As steam pressure builds, the engine speeds up, which causes the weights on a flywheel to fly outward due to increasing centrifugal force. As the weights fly outward, the governor's valve is opened, allowing steam to escape. As steam escapes, the pressure declines, slowing down the engine. The reduction in speed reduces the centrifugal force, allowing the weights to retract, and the valve to close. We observe the same phenomenon with the cruise control on a car as the incline angle of the road changes. In more complex systems, such as economic or ecological systems, oscillations caused by the balancing effect of negative feedback loops can fluctuate widely, and extend to long durations, as for example with business cycles in economic systems, or the swings in the relative population sizes of predator and prey species.

quality, which reduces the quality gap, and prompts a reduction in the level of investment in capacity. However, there can be a significant delay in the company's provision of support capacity, due to its inability to anticipate its needs on a timely basis, and the time it takes to train new technicians.

Taken together, loops B2 and B3 form a figure-8 reinforcing loop (the figure-8 has an even number of negative signs). If the company does not anticipate and respond to its service capacity needs in a timely manner, it can find itself in a situation in which it will experience a continual downward spiral in both product demand and service quality. For example, chronic underinvestment in service capacity will shift the system's dynamics from a sales-growth state where the dominant loop is R1, to a sales-decline state where the dominant loop is the B2/B3 figure-8 with a continual downward pressure on sales.[48] Also, a shift could occur if the company fails to account for the time lag between investment and implementation of additional support capacity. For example, the company might target its service capacity needs to a current level of product demand, but before the capacity is installed (due to the delay), demand drops further. Once the additional service capacity is implemented, the company finds it has excess capacity and reduces it to the level needed to service the new lower demand.

To better anticipate its technical support capacity needs, the company could implement customer service standards and use KPIs to track process performance and customer satisfaction. Of course, as the company implements its expansion strategy, these quality standards might need to be changed for the new markets. For example, moving into a new broad corporate market could place even more stress on the technical support process, since new corporate users might not be as technically competent as are existing technically-knowledgeable customers.

An understanding of these systems dynamics makes it apparent that the company's new strategy involves a difficult balancing act in terms of choices about where to apply investment funds. Sales growth imposes additional stress on service quality, which, if left unattended, will negatively impact product demand through a deteriorating service reputation.

---

48 The ability to shift loop dominance is a characteristic of nonlinear systems. A given equation in a system of nonlinear differential equations does not constantly apply at all times. In fact, nonlinear models have the property that they change their active structure over time. A linear system does not have the property of being able to change its structure endogenously. Unfortunately, nonlinear systems are not only hard to estimate statistically, but are usually impossible to solve in closed form. For this reason, systems theorists support the analysis of nonlinear systems using simulation methods.

Also, expansion into new markets, especially overseas markets, involves a complicated and costly web of marketing and shipping arrangements that will require substantial up-front investment. In addition, expansion into a broader domestic corporate market will impose additional stress on the technical support process, and necessitate further investment in technical support capacity.

If these two strategic goals were both pursued aggressively, we would expect profit margins to suffer in the short run. If management overreacts to a short run decline in profit margin by reducing technical support capacity, the result could be further declines in service quality and product demand. If the auditor obtains the KPIs related to customer service process performance and service quality that are used by the company to monitor and manage its service quality and capacity,[49] and if, in his judgment, the related standards used by management to make service capacity investments are appropriate, he will have obtained audit evidence to support his expectation about the validity of the reported profit margin.[50] That is, KPIs can provide assurance to the auditor that the organization is maintaining the level of process quality required to sustain product demand.

At the conclusion of the audit, the BMP auditor will have constructed a fully integrated client business model containing all of the information he has collected and integrated through the application of the four BMP measurement principles described above and through his mental or more formal business simulation processes. He will use the completed model as the basis for his final review of the adjusted financial statements and his final assessment of the entity's ability to continue as a going concern. Also, as discussed next, the client business model will provide a basis for the auditor's provision of additional assurance to management about the entity's achieved level of performance in terms of its operational, financial reporting, and compliance objectives and goals.

BMP Continuous Improvement

An organization, like any other living system, controls and improves its operating performance and its productive potential by looping successively

---

49 KPMG has developed a database and technology tool it calls the Global Benchmarking System (GBS) to assist the auditor's acquisition of data and knowledge related to process-specific and entity-wide key performance indicators. GBS's international and industry-segmented databases contain entity-level KPIs, e.g., the ratios that comprise the ROE tree, and process-level KPIs, for samples of both public and private companies located around the world. Industry averages and other descriptive statistics, and "best-practice" performance standards are also included in the databases. These databases are updated as soon as new KPI data become available.

50 Of course, the auditor's expectation can be based on other evidence sources as well. Other sources might include other analytical procedures (e.g., ratio analyses), other KPI analyses (e.g., KPIs used by management to measure the effectiveness of the inventory management process), sales cutoff tests, etc.

through a process involving measurement and reporting of performance feedback, innovation, and implementation of new and improved technologies and organizational designs. Over time, the rapidity of adaptive behavior increases as organizations, and the broader systems they are open to, become more connected, more complex, and therefore more nimble.

Exhibit 14 [p. 60] depicts an organization's process of adaptation using a feedback loop diagram. As illustrated in Exhibit 14, at its inception, the organization adopts a mission and defines its business strategy. It then defines its business objectives, implements an organizational design and related business controls, conducts business activities, and measures and reports operational outcomes. Actual outcomes then are compared to desired outcomes specified in the organization's strategic plan. Knowledge about observed gaps, integrated with knowledge about observed environmental changes, triggers organizational learning, innovation of new technologies, and their implementation. The organization cycles through the loop on a continuous basis, reacting to day-to-day operational feedback by making modest, short-run operational changes, and reacting in a more fundamental and contemplative way to feedback about system-wide performance and system-wide risks. Typical reactions would include reorienting the business strategy, and redesigning business processes so that they become consistent with the new vision and business objectives.

Being an open system, the behavior of the organization triggers changes in its external environment as well, through its interactions with outsiders. For example, customers' tastes and preferences are impacted by the introduction of new products, and by the organization's implementation of new technologies that impact product quality and price, and service quality and cost. Also, capital suppliers adapt their strategies and behaviors based on feedback received from the organization and other feedback about the economic environment that changes their perceptions about the rank order of alternative investment opportunities. As depicted in Exhibit 14, the external auditor's traditional role has been to provide assurance to capital suppliers and regulators about the validity of the assertions embodied in the entity's financial statements. Also, in the management letter the auditor typically would provide some independent, but limited, feedback about the quality of the entity's information management process, especially in terms of its effectiveness at producing financial information for external users. In this capacity, the external auditor plays an important role in the broader economy-wide system of feedback and control, but plays a lesser role in the feedback and control processes inside the organization.

Having developed an in-depth understanding of the client's business and industry, the BMP auditor is in a unique position to serve a valuable role in the organization's internal feedback processes, as well as in the larger economic system's feedback process. Exhibit 15 depicts some of these new feedback roles and assurance opportunities. The in-depth knowledge the BMP auditor acquires about external forces and macroeconomic trends, the organization's strategic and process risks, the quality and efficiency of the strategic management, core business, and resource management processes, combined with the key process performance indicators he collects, equip the BMP auditor to provide valuable, independent feedback to the organization's board of directors, upper management, and business process owners as a by-product of the BMP audit.

When an individual looks in a mirror, at a photograph, or at a video tape of himself in the act of performing a task, the externally produced reflection of his image, appearance, or performance can differ significantly from the prior image that he had formed through self-reflection — the image formed in the mind's eye. Moreover, the externally produced image can provide new insights that trigger the individual's learning and adaptation. For example,

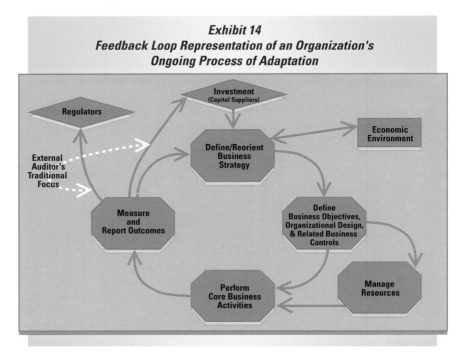

**Exhibit 14
Feedback Loop Representation of an Organization's
Ongoing Process of Adaptation**

public speaking instructors often use video tape to present an accurate reflection of an individual student's performance, enabling the student to perceive and internalize his weaknesses so that he can adapt his techniques to enhance his performance. Or, a football coach might use video tape to illustrate to his players certain tactical mistakes the implications of which cannot be readily visualized without the benefit of a broad-based, external view of the formation and execution of the whole play.

Similarly, an organization's image of itself formed through the process of self-reflection can be significantly biased. This bias can arise unintentionally via the organization's internal mediating processes, and the stresses arising from interactions among its sub-units and between its sub-units and external economic agents. For example, incentives and rewards used to motivate and focus the behaviors of managers and employees also can motivate these internal agents to misrepresent important feedback, especially when it would otherwise reflect negative, or sub-goal, performance. Or, managers and process owners who have invested their reputations and past

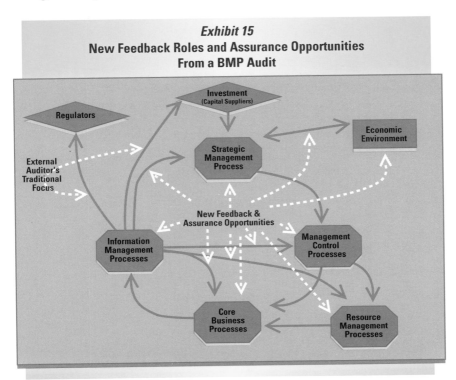

Exhibit 15
New Feedback Roles and Assurance Opportunities
From a BMP Audit

energies in specific projects or technologies sometimes try to avert risk or avoid change by misrepresenting project-related risks and outcomes. And, sometimes project or process risks and outcomes are misrepresented unintentionally due to limitations inherent in human information processing.

These are among the reasons that managers can benefit from independent feedback and assurances provided by the external auditor.[51] The BMP auditor is equipped to paint a picture for directors, managers, and process owners that reflects an independent image of aspects of a) entity-level performance, b) structural strengths and weaknesses, c) business process strengths and weaknesses, and d) its current strategic positioning and possible vulnerabilities related to emerging trends.

The dashed arrows presented in the center of Exhibit 15 point to a variety of possibilities for the BMP auditor to serve valuable intraorganization feedback or assurance roles. First, note that Exhibit 15 includes three additional intraorganization feedback lines (solid lines) from the information management process back to the management control, resource management, and core business processes to depict the internal reporting of performance information. Exhibit 15 further identifies two broad classes of BMP audit by-products: opportunities for the BMP auditor to provide assurance about the quality of internal information (dashed lines pointing to intraorganization feedback lines); and opportunities for the BMP auditor to provide supplemental feedback to managers and process owners about residual strategic and process risks, key performance indicators, emerging business risks, and process and control structure vulnerabilities (dashed lines pointing to the internal processes themselves, and to the external environment).

In the next section, we discuss our views about how complex analytical procedures comprising a client business model, and KPIs for key business processes and the entity taken as a whole, provide audit evidence about the validity of financial-statement assertions.

---

[51] The report of the AICPA Special Committee on Assurance Services (also called the Elliott Commitee, Home Page address, http://www.aicpa.org/assurance /pre/index.htm) provides a more complete discussion of the value of assurance services from both internal and external to the organization perspectives. This report also discusses attestation services for assertions other than those contained within financial statements.

8 Business Models, KPIs, Expectations, and Audit Evidence

How do we use the information gleaned about the parts to build up a theory of the whole? The deep difficulty here lies in the fact that the complex whole may exhibit properties that are not readily explained by understanding the parts. The complex whole, in a completely nonmystical sense, can often exhibit collective properties, "emergent" features that are lawful in their own right.

Stuart Kauffman

At Home in the Universe: The Search for the Laws of Self-Organization and Complexity [52]

External auditing effectively involves developing expectations about business performance and financial position, comparing the expectations to assertions[53] embodied in the financial statements, and evaluating significant differences. Expectations should be developed by integrating information from reliable sources into expert knowledge about the entity's behavior that underlies the representations made by management in the financial statements. And expectations should not be unduly influenced by the very assertions being audited. Otherwise, audit conclusions can be biased toward acceptance of the assertions whether or not they are valid.

In the traditional detailed audit, some of the auditor's expectations are developed by selecting a random or judgmental sample of accounting transactions; testing the transactions through inspection and validation of corroborating documentation, observation, inquiry, or recomputation; and projecting the adjusted sample amount to a population basis. The projection then is compared to the recorded account balance, and the difference, if material, triggers further evaluation or the recording of an adjustment to the account balance.

---

52 Stuart Kauffman, *At Home in the Universe: The Search for the Laws of Self-Organization and Complexity* (Oxford University Press, New York, Oxford, 1995).

53 According to AU Section 326.03, "Assertions are representations by management that are embodied in financial statement components. They can be either explicit or implicit and can be classified according to the following broad categories: existence or occurrence, completeness, rights and obligations, valuation or allocation, and presentation and disclosure." Of course, one could classify management's representations differently. For example, a financial statement user interested in an organization's strategic performance might be most interested in combinations of financial statement components to better understand the entity's past and prospective strategic performance – management representations implicit in measures such as return on equity and its component drivers: asset utilization, operating efficiency, and financial leverage.

Expectations developed from details of transaction samples, because they are based on a reductionist process, have inherent shortcomings which can lead to potential decision-making biases[54]. For example, if during a detailed audit of transactions, the auditor gains an understanding of the business primarily by reviewing a sample of accounting transactions and inspecting and validating corroborating documents, he may be predisposed to assume, perhaps erroneously, that the economics underlying the client's business activities are reflected accurately and completely in these accounting transactions. Of course, such a predisposition could bias the auditor's judgment in favor of accepting the entity-level management assertions. Also, such a narrow perspective could cause the auditor to inadvertently truncate his auditing procedures before he has collected a sufficient amount of evidence[55]. Without a more thorough and unbiased understanding of the inherent business risks that threaten the client's business activities, the auditor's ability to judge effectively whether sufficient competent evidential matter has been collected can be hindered.

As implied in the authoritative guidance, an auditor needs a sound and comprehensive understanding of the client's business and industry to develop valid expectations about financial-statement assertions and to provide the kind of insight that will *heighten his professional skepticism* when assertions and expectations do not articulate. It is unlikely that an auditor will be able to ascertain the extent to which client business risks are being controlled by limiting his investigation to the information processing controls embedded in the client's accounting system. Without looking outside of that system it is difficult for the auditor to learn whether it processes all business activities and measures them giving due consideration to all relevant business risks. Also, for the auditor to judge effectively whether accounting estimates and valuations reflect the proper levels of uncontrolled business risk, he must look outside of the accounting system to the actual sources of risks, and the processes in place to control them.

---

54 This discussion is in no way meant to imply that detailed transactions testing is of limited or no value. Indeed, such testing plays a valuable and necessary role in the performance of an external audit. One very important advantage of detailed transactions testing is that under the right conditions (e.g., random sampling) the precision of the expectation can be quantified easily. The current discussion focuses on the need to develop expectations at the entity level – expectations that are not influenced significantly by the assertions being audited and that relate to the client organization's strategic fit within its broader economic system, and its process performance within this strategic context.

55 For example, recall the LSL study cited earlier in the monograph. In the study, the researchers stated: "Based on a review of depositions and audit workpapers, it is our view that an understanding of the economic factors surrounding one of Lincoln's main source of profits during this period, sales of undeveloped land, was not adequately integrated with the detailed evidence they obtained. . . . [T]he auditor's transaction approach to the audit appears to have inhibited their consideration of the economic reasonableness of transactions." Merle M. Erickson, Brian W. Mayhew, and William L. Felix, Jr., "Understanding the Client's Business: Lessons from Lincoln Savings and Loan," unpublished working paper (1996).

Exhibit 16 [p. 66] presents the relationships between strategic-systems business modeling and business-process-focused analytical procedures, and the client's key business activities, related inherent business risks, business processes, and audit risk. As shown on the far-left side of Exhibit 16, an organization's business activities present inherent business risks[56] that if not controlled, can significantly impact audit risk. Business controls are embedded in the client's business processes to reduce these business risks to acceptable levels. The BMP auditor uses the complex strategy-, and business-process-oriented, system of analytical procedures described earlier to develop evidential matter that provides support for his expectations about financial-statement assertions. These procedures also direct the auditor's attention to those specific transactions and account balances that warrant further testing using a combined strategic-systems and traditional reductionist testing approach. Exhibit 16 presents the five general categories of the client's business activities to which these analytical procedures are applied. As discussed in earlier sections of the monograph, these activities and related business processes are:

- *business strategy* – the strategic management process sets business strategies, monitors the environment for strategic risks, and reorients strategies when warranted;

- *business objectives and organizational design* – management control processes set and control business objectives and design the management and operational structures of the organization to execute the business strategy; risk monitoring and management controls are embedded in the core business and resource management processes to monitor and control process performance as it relates to the organization's strategy;

- *core business activities* – core business processes perform core business activities;

- *resource management activities* – resource management processes manage the human, physical, and financial resources utilized by the entity; and

---

56 SAS No. 47, *Audit Risk and Materiality in Conducting an Audit* [para. 20] defines inherent risk as "the susceptibility of an assertion to a material misstatement, assuming that there are no related internal control structure policies or procedures." Generally speaking, these inherent risks are client business risks. For example, SAS No. 47 [para. 20 a] suggests that accounts consisting of amounts derived from accounting estimates pose greater inherent risks than do accounts consisting of relatively routine, factual data, and that external factors also influence inherent risk.

• *information management* – the information management process captures and reports, both internally and externally, outcomes resulting from all business activities, and information about residual business risks related to the organization's strategies and process performance.

The five corresponding analytical processes presented in Exhibit 16 – strategic analysis; business modeling; core business process analysis; resource management process analysis; and information management process analysis – combined with the articulation of business measurements (KPIs) of process and entity-level performance, comprise an ensemble of analytical procedures rooted in the strategic-systems perspective.

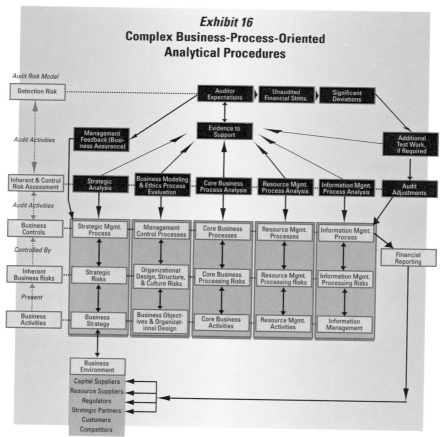

Exhibit 16
Complex Business-Process-Oriented Analytical Procedures

Analytical procedures, by their very nature, are complex and require an adequate understanding of business activities and other underlying economic phenomena. Exhibit 17 [p. 68] provides an overview of strategic-systems analytical procedures. The exhibit shows that auditing the organization through a strategic-systems lens, like that provided by BMP, entails integration and assimilation of knowledge of the organization's business and industry to develop expectations from a "whole-system" perspective. Just as a painter uses separate methods, images, tones, and techniques to create his "whole" vision on canvas, the strategic-systems auditor uses process analyses and business measurements to create a "whole system" frame of the client's performance and financial position. As shown in Exhibit 17, when auditing an organization's financial statements through a strategic-systems lens, the auditor develops an understanding of the client's business strategies and related industry and market niches, and identifies the external forces that threaten the success of these strategies. Using this knowledge, he identifies the key competencies and related business processes that drive the organization's implementation of its strategy and its interactions with its environment.

Next, the auditor identifies the key sub-processes for each of these key business processes and he studies these sub-processes to gain an understanding of their objectives, inputs, activities, outputs, and supporting systems. He uses this knowledge to identify business process risks – risks that threaten the attainment of process objectives – and as a decision frame to evaluate business controls where warranted[57]. At each sub-process he also assesses information risks – the risks related to the information needs of the organization, including its financial reporting and other compliance reporting needs, and its information needs for the efficient and effective performance of its other key processes and sub-processes. Using his assessments of information risks as a decision frame, the auditor evaluates information processing controls and tests certain controls where warranted.

Also, during sub-process analysis the strategic-systems auditor assesses the alignments between activities, sub-processes, core business processes, and business strategies to understand whether internal activities and process objectives are properly aligned with the business strategy. For each key business process, residual risks are linked to financial-statement assertions (assertions related to strategic performance, and sub-unit assertions at the account balance or class of transactions level, with further subclassification as either routine transactions, nonroutine transactions, or accounting estimates).

---

57 AU Section 319, *Consideration of the Internal Control Structure in a Financial Statement Audit* states "The ultimate purpose of assessing control risk is to contribute to the auditor's evaluation of the risk that material misstatements exist in the financial statements. The process of assessing control risk (together with assessing inherent risk) *provides evidential matter* about the risk that such misstatements may exist in the financial statements" [para. 79, 1997] [emphasis added].

Next, the auditor uses his knowledge of those competencies and processes that are critical to the successful implementation of the client's strategy to identify and measure process KPIs. Once each key business process has been analyzed in this fashion, the residual risks for each process, taken together with the key performance indicators and other relevant business knowledge, are combined by financial-statement assertion to develop an integrated view of the validity of each assertion. For each assertion, this combined knowledge about activities, risks, controls, and process performance is evaluated to identify potential inconsistencies. Entity-level key performance indicators, e.g., ratios that are components of the ROE-tree,[58] account-balance and ratio trend analysis, and common-size financial statements, are measured and articulated with the combined business process, risk, control, and KPI information. The entity-level KPIs also are evaluated in terms of their consistency with the organization's business strategy, and the possible impacts of external forces that threaten the success of their strategy.

Through the application of strategic-systems-oriented analytical procedures and the related knowledge-assimilation process presented in Exhibit

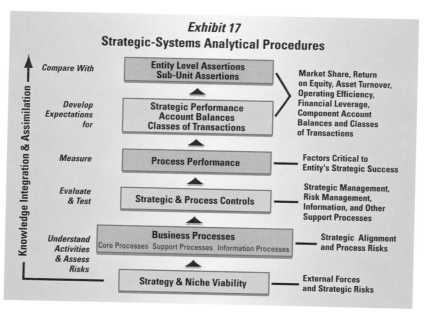

Exhibit 17
Strategic-Systems Analytical Procedures

Knowledge Integration & Assimilation

Compare With	Entity Level Assertions / Sub-Unit Assertions	Market Share, Return on Equity, Asset Turnover, Operating Efficiency, Financial Leverage, Component Account Balances and Classes of Transactions
Develop Expectations for	Strategic Performance / Account Balances / Classes of Transactions	
Measure	Process Performance	Factors Critical to Entity's Strategic Success
Evaluate & Test	Strategic & Process Controls	Strategic Management, Risk Management, Information, and Other Support Processes
Understand Activities & Assess Risks	Business Processes / Core Processes Support Processes Information Processes	Strategic Alignment and Process Risks
	Strategy & Niche Viability	External Forces and Strategic Risks

---

[58] The return-on-equity (ROE) tree is a decomposition of the return on equity ratio into components representing asset utilization, operating efficiency, and financial leverage.

17, the auditor gathers, analyzes, and integrates *reliable* and *independent* information which becomes *expert knowledge*. Such expert knowledge, in turn, enables the auditor *to reach valid and defensible conclusions* about the appropriateness of financial-statement assertions.[59] The sources of much of this expert business knowledge reside outside of the accounting and finance areas, making them more independent and reliable than the sources within the accounting function which traditionally have been the subjects of audit inquiries.

Finally, AU Section 316, *Consideration of Fraud in a Financial Statement Audit*, states: "The auditor should specifically assess the risk of material misstatement of the financial statements due to fraud and should consider that assessment in designing the audit procedures to be performed" [AU 316.12, 1997]. The use of the complex analytical procedures comprising a strategic-systems-based knowledge acquisition framework, coupled with an assessment of other fraud risk factors such as those factors presented in AU Section 316, should improve the auditor's ability to detect and diagnose anomalies associated with management fraud. And, a comprehensive business knowledge decision frame will serve to heighten the auditor's level of professional skepticism when appropriate, e.g., by enabling the auditor to develop his own hypotheses about unusual financial-statement trends and fluctuations without relying exclusively on management's explanations.

To summarize, through their inherent construct validity, strategic-systems-based analytical procedures, like those performed by the BMP auditor, provide evidence on the:

- inherent business risks and their potential impact on financial-statement assertions in the absence of adequate controls;

- business control risks, i.e., residual inherent business risks and their potential impact on financial-statement assertions;

- specific financial-statement assertions such as the valuations and assumptions underlying difficult-to-audit accounting estimates and nonroutine transactions;

---

59 The authoritative guidance on external auditing defines *evidential matter* that supports the financial statements as the "underlying accounting data and all corroborating information available to the auditor" [AU 326.15]. Paragraph 17 of SAS No. 80 defines corroborating evidence as follows: Corroborating evidential matter includes both written and electronic information such as checks; records of electronic funds transfers; invoices; contracts; minutes of meetings; confirmations and other written representations by knowledgeable people; information obtained by the auditor from inquiry, observation, inspection, and physical examination; and *other information developed by, or available to, the auditor which permits him or her to reach conclusions through valid reasoning* [AU 326.17; emphasis added].

- information processing risks related to the processing of routine transactions;

- achieved level of business performance at the entity level;

- achieved level of business performance at the business process levels;

- entity's ability to generate future cash flows;

- quality and permanence of the entity's reported earnings; and

- value of the company.

9 Concluding Comments

In a period of rapid change, it is the adaptable, not the well-adapted, that survive. Foresight always wins in the long run. Reacting to problems means letting the system control us. Only by using foresight do we have a real chance to control the system. Those who do not try to create the future they want must endure the future they get.

Draper L. Kauffman, Jr.
An Introduction to Systems Thinking[60]

The risk-based strategic-systems audit approach, described in some detail in this monograph, is an innovative and powerful means of meeting external audit goals as well as intra-organizational assurance objectives. Admittedly, however, it retains much of what is now conventional in external auditing. The risk-based strategic-systems auditor still embraces the audit risk model; still allocates audit effort on the basis of risk assessments; still performs procedures that, for the most part, would be familiar to conventional auditors; and still formulates an opinion on the financial statements based on the resulting evidence. Indeed, what is innovative about a risk-based strategic-systems audit lies elsewhere. Specifically, it conditions the auditor's expectations on knowledge from perspectives gleaned from a marriage of the fields of auditing, systems theory, and business strategy. These knowledge-laden expectations form the basis of a new breed of analytical procedures that hold promise for highly effective audits.

Exhibit 18 [p. 72] contrasts the traditional reductionist audit approach with a risk-based strategic-systems audit approach like BMP. The reductionist approach assumes that accounting and auditing knowledge plays the primary role in forming audit judgments, and implicitly de-emphasizes the role of knowledge about the business. The risk-based strategic-systems approach reflects the systems-thinking view that to audit assertions effectively, the auditor must comprehend the client's whole business environment and interpret the role of significant transactions from this business knowledge frame — the broader context infuses meaning into the parts.

---

60 Quotes paraphrased from Draper L. Kauffman, Jr., *Systems One: An Introduction to Systems Thinking* (Future Systems, Inc., S. A. Carlton, Publisher, Minneapolis, 1980). Originally entitled *The Human Environment: An Introduction to Environmental Systems*, developed under a grant from the U.S. Department of Health, Education, and Welfare.

Exhibit 18
Comparison of Reductionist and
Strategic-Systems Audit Approaches

Reductionist Audit Approach	*Strategic-Systems Audit Approach*
Transaction Orientation Based on the notion that the whole can be discerned by examining the parts	**Holistic Orientation** Based on the belief that the broader context infuses meaning into the parts
Focus on the Information Process Through an understanding of the interrelationships among reported information, one is able to develop a sound expectation model about performance	**Focus on the Business Processes** Presumes the objectives of the business strategy are delivered through key processes; therefore a sound expectation model must be based on a review of strategy and process indicators
Expert Knowledge of Accounting and Auditing Relies on in-depth understanding of auditing procedures and accounting rules predominantly to enable the attester to verify consistencies and detect anomalies	**Expert Knowledge of Business** Considers a broader understanding of the entity and its environment to contribute significantly to the attester's ability to verify consistencies and detect anomalies
Discrete Systems Comprehends systems as disconnected from one another, generating unrelated transactions that can be reviewed by individuals working independently	**Networked** Understands the organization as a dynamic network whose systems cannot be examined in isolation
Audit Risk Based on belief that opinions about financial statements can be issued independently from a commentary on the client business risk	**Business Risk** Considers the financial-statement opinion to be inextricably connected to a broader assessment of client business risk

Appendix

Excerpts from the U.S. Statements on Auditing Standards (SAS) Dealing with Judgment and Obtaining an Understanding of the Client's Business

AU Section 110 — *Responsibilities and Functions of the Independent Auditor*

• In the observance of generally accepted auditing standards, the independent auditor must exercise his judgment in determining which auditing procedures are necessary in the circumstances to afford a reasonable basis for his opinion. His judgment is required to be the informed judgment of a qualified professional person [AU 110.04, 1997].

AU Section 210 — *Training and Proficiency of the Independent Auditor*

• It should be recognized that the training of a professional man includes a continual awareness of developments taking place in business and in his profession [AU 210.04, 1997].

• In the course of his day-to-day practice, the independent auditor encounters a wide range of judgment on the part of management, varying from true objective judgment to the occasional extreme of deliberate misstatement. He is retained to audit and report upon the financial statements of a business because, through his training and experience, he has become skilled in accounting and auditing and has acquired the ability to consider objectively and to exercise independent judgment with respect to the information recorded in books of account or otherwise disclosed by his audit [AU 210.05, 1997].

AU Section 311 — *Planning and Supervision*

• The nature, extent, and timing of planning vary with the size and complexity of the entity, experience with the entity, and knowledge of the entity's business [AU 311.03, 1997].

• The auditor should obtain a level of knowledge of the entity's business that will enable him to plan and perform his audit in accordance with generally accepted auditing standards. That level of knowledge should enable him to obtain an understanding of the events, transactions, and practices that, in his judgment, may have a significant effect on the financial statements. . . . Knowledge of the entity's business helps the auditor in:

a. Identifying areas that may need special consideration.

b. Assessing conditions under which accounting data are produced, processed, reviewed, and accumulated within the organization.

c. Evaluating the reasonableness of estimates, such as valuation of inventories, depreciation, allowances for doubtful accounts, and percentage of completion of long-term contracts.

d. Evaluating the reasonableness of management representations.

e. Making judgments about the appropriateness of the accounting principles applied and the adequacy of disclosures [AU 311.06, 1997]

• The auditor should obtain a knowledge of matters that relate to the nature of the entity's business, its organization, and its operating characteristics. Such matters include, for example, the type of business, types of products and services, capital structure, related parties, locations, and production, distribution, and compensation methods. The auditor should also consider matters affecting the industry in which the entity operates, such as economic conditions, government regulations, and changes in technology, as they relate to his audit. Other matters, such as accounting practices common to the industry, competitive conditions, and, if available, financial trends and ratios should also be considered by the auditor [AU 311.07, 1997].

• Knowledge of an entity's business is ordinarily obtained through experience with the entity or its industry and inquiry of personnel of the entity. Working papers from prior years may contain useful information about the nature of the business, organizational structure, operating characteristics, and transactions that may require special consideration. Other sources an auditor may consult include AICPA accounting and audit guides, industry publications, financial statements of other entities in the industry, textbooks, periodicals, and individuals knowledgeable about the industry [AU 311.08, 1997].

AU Section 312 — *Audit Risk and Materiality in Conducting an Audit*

• According to section 311, the nature, timing, and extent of planning and thus of the considerations of audit risk and materiality vary with the size and complexity of the entity, auditor's experience with the entity, and his knowledge of the entity's business [AU 312.11, 1997].

AU Section 316a — The Auditor's Responsibility to Detect and Report Errors and Irregularities

• An assessment of the risk of material misstatements should be made during planning. The auditor's understanding of internal control should either heighten or mitigate the auditor's concern about the risk of material misstatements. The factors considered in assessing risk should be considered in combination to make an overall judgment; the presence of some factors in isolation would not necessarily indicate increased risk. Factors such as those listed below may be considered.

Management Characteristics

- • Management operating and financing decisions are dominated by a single person.

- • Management's attitude toward financial reporting is unduly aggressive.

- • Management (particularly senior accounting personnel) turnover is high.

- • Management places undue emphasis on meeting earnings projections.

- • Management's reputation in the business community is poor.

Operating and Industry Characteristics

- • Profitability of entity relative to its industry is inadequate or inconsistent.

- • Sensitivity of operating results to economic factors (inflation, interest rates, unemployment, etc.) is high.

- • Rate of change in entity's industry is rapid.

- • Direction of change in entity's industry is declining with many business failures.

- • Organization is decentralized without adequate monitoring.

- • Internal or external matters that raise substantial doubt about the entity's ability to continue as a going concern are present. (See section 341, *The Auditor's Consideration of an Entity's Ability to Continue as a Going Concern.*)

Engagement Characteristics

- Many contentious or difficult accounting issues are present.

- Significant difficult-to-audit transactions or balances are present.

- Significant and unusual related party transactions not in the ordinary course of business are present.

- Nature, cause (if known), or the amount of known and likely misstatements detected in the audit of prior period's financial statements is significant.

- It is a new client with no prior history or sufficient information is not available from the predecessor auditor [AU 316.10, 1997].

AU Section 319 — *Consideration of Internal Control in a Financial Statement Audit*

- The five components of internal control are applicable to the audit of every entity. The components should be considered in the context of:

  - The entity's size.

  - The entity's organization and ownership characteristics.

  - The nature of the entity's business.

  - The diversity and complexity of the entity's operations.

  - The entity's methods of transmitting, processing, maintaining, and accessing information.

  - Applicable legal and regulatory requirements [AU 319.15, 1997].

- Risks relevant to financial reporting include external and internal events and circumstances that may occur and adversely affect an entity's ability to record, process, summarize, and report financial data consistent with the assertions of management in the financial statements. Risks can arise or change due to circumstances such as the following:

  - Changes in operating environment

  - New personnel

  - New or revamped information systems

  - Rapid growth

- New technology

- New lines, products, or activities

- Corporate restructurings

- Foreign operations

- Accounting pronouncements [AU 319.29, 1997].

AU Section 326 — *Evidential Matter*

- In obtaining evidential matter in support of financial statement assertions, the auditor develops specific audit objectives in the light of those assertions. In developing the audit objectives of a particular engagement, the auditor should consider the specific circumstances of the entity, including the nature of its economic activity and the accounting practices unique to its industry [AU 326.09, 1997].

AU Section 329 — *Analytical Procedures*

- Understanding financial relationships is essential in planning and evaluating the results of analytical procedures, and generally requires knowledge of the client and the industry or industries in which the client operates [AU 329.03, 1997].

- Analytical procedures involve comparisons of recorded amounts, or ratios developed from recorded amounts, to expectations developed by the auditor. The auditor develops such expectations by identifying and using plausible relationships that are reasonably expected to exist based on the auditor's understanding of the client and of the industry in which the client operates [AU 329.05, 1997].

AU Section 334 — *Related Parties*

- In the absence of evidence to the contrary, transactions with related parties should not be assumed to be outside the ordinary course of business. The auditor should, however, be aware of the possibility that transactions with related parties may have been motivated solely, or in large measure, by conditions similar to the following:

  - Lack of sufficient working capital or credit to continue in business

  - An urgent desire for a continued favorable earnings record in the hope of supporting the price of the company's stock

  - An overly optimistic earnings forecast

- Dependence on a single or relatively few products, customers, or transactions for the continuing success of the venture

- A declining industry characterized by a large number of business failures

- Excess capacity

- Significant litigation, especially litigation between stockholders and management

- Significant obsolescence dangers because the company is in a high technology industry [AU 334.06, 1997].

- After identifying related party transactions, the auditor should apply the procedures he considers necessary to obtain satisfaction concerning the purpose, nature, and extent of these transactions and their effect on the financial statements. The procedures should be directed toward obtaining and evaluating sufficient competent evidential matter and should extend beyond inquiry of management. Procedures that should be considered include the following:

- Obtain an understanding of the business purpose of the transaction [AU 334.09, 1997].

AU Section 341 — *The Auditor's Consideration of an Entity's Ability to Continue as a Going Concern*

- In performing audit procedures such as those presented in paragraph .05, the auditor may identify information about certain conditions or events that, when considered in the aggregate, indicate there could be substantial doubt about the entity's ability to continue as a going concern for a reasonable period of time. The significance of such conditions and events will depend on the circumstances, and some may have significance only when viewed in conjunction with others. The following are examples of such conditions and events:

- Negative trends — for example, recurring operating losses, working capital deficiencies, negative cash flows from operating activities, adverse key financial ratios

- Other indications of possible financial difficulties — for example, default on loan or similar agreements, arrearages in dividends, denial of usual trade credit from suppliers, restructuring of debt, noncompliance with statutory capital requirements, need to seek new sources or methods of financing or to dispose of substantial assets

- Internal matters — for example, work stoppages or other labor difficulties, substantial dependence on the success of a particular project, uneconomic long-term commitments, need to significantly revise operations

- External matters that have occurred — for example, legal proceedings, legislation, or similar matters that might jeopardize an entity's ability to operate; loss of a key franchise, license, or patent; loss of a principal, customer, or supplier; uninsured or underinsured catastrophe such as a drought, earthquake, or flood [AU 341.06, 1997].

References

Ackoff, R., *Concept of Corporate Planning* (John Wiley & Sons, New York, 1970).

Ackoff, R., *Redesigning the Future* (John Wiley & Sons, New York, 1980).

Ackoff, R., *The Democratic Corporation* (Oxford University Press, New York, 1992).

AICPA, *Codification of Statements on Auditing Standards* (AICPA, New York, 1997).

AICPA, Special Committee on Assurance Services Home Page, http://www.aicpa.org/assurance/pre/index.htm.

Anderson, V., and L. Johnson, *Systems Thinking Basics: From Concepts to Causal Loops* (Pegasus Communications, Inc., Cambridge, MA, 1997).

Andrews, K. R., *The Concept of Corporate Strategy* (Dow Jones-Irwin, New York, 1971).

Beer, S., *Decision and Control: The Meaning of Operational Research and Management Cybernetics* (John Wiley and Sons, London, 1966).

Beer, S., *Platform for Change* (John Wiley and Sons, London, 1975).

Beer, S., *Brain of the Firm: The Managerial Cybernetics of Organization* (John Wiley and Sons, Chichester, England, 1981).

Bell, T. B., and A. M. Wright, eds., *Auditing Practice, Research, and Education: A Productive Collaboration* (AICPA, New York, 1995).

Brandenburger, A., and B. Nalebuff, *Co-Opetition* (Doubleday, New York, 1996).

Brickley, J. A., C. W. Smith, and J. L. Zimmerman, *Organizational Architecture: A Managerial Economics Approach* (Richard D. Irwin, New York, 1996).

Campbell, A., M. Devine, and D. Young, *A Sense of Mission* (Economist Books, London, 1990).

Capra, F., *The Turning Point — Science, Society, and the Rising Culture* (Bantam Books, New York, 1982).

Champy, J., and M. Hammer, *Reengineering the Corporation: A Manifesto for Business Revolution* (HarperBusiness, New York, 1993).

Collins, D. J., and C. A. Montgomery, "Competing on Resources: Strategy in the 1990s," *Harvard Business Review* 73 (July/Aug 1995), pp. 118-128.

Collins, J., and T. Ruefli, *Strategic Risk: A State-Defined Approach* (Kluwer Academic Publishers, Norwell, MA, 1996).

Collins, J. C. and J. I. Porras, *Built to Last: Successful Habits of Visionary Companies* (HarperCollins, New York, 1994).

De Geus, Arie, *The Living Company* (Harvard Business School Press, Boston, 1997).

Depew, D. J., and B. H. Weber, "Evolution, Ethics, and the Complexity Revolution," *Evolution and Human Values,* Robert Wesson and Patricia A. Williams, eds. (Rodipi, Amsterdam and Atlanta, GA, 1995), pp. 49 - 77.

Erickson, M. M., B. W. Mayhew, and W. L. Felix, Jr., "Understanding the Client's Business: Lessons from Lincoln Savings and Loan," unpublished working paper (1996).

Forrester, J. W., *Industrial Dynamics* (MIT Press, Cambridge, MA, 1961).

Gorman, P., M. Pruett, and H. Thomas, "Development of Competitive Strategies," *Concise International Encyclopedia of Business and Management,* Malcolm Warner, ed. (Routledge, London and New York, 1996), pp. 692 - 710.

Hagel, J. III, and A. G. Armstrong, *Net Gain: Expanding Markets Through Virtual Communities* (Harvard Business School Press, Boston, 1997).

Hamel, G., "Strategy As Revolution," *Harvard Business Review* 74 (July/Aug 1996), pp. 69-82.

Hamel, G., and C. K. Prahalad, "Strategic Intent," *Harvard Business Review* 67 (May/June, 1989), pp. 63 - 76.

Hamel, G., and C. K. Prahalad, *Competing for the Future* (Harvard Business School Press, Boston, 1994).

Hock, D. W., "Institutions in the Age of Mindcrafting," presented at the Bionomics Annual Conference, San Francisco, October 22, 1994: reproduced with permission by Cascade Policy Institute, and accessible from their web site "www.cascadepolicy.org/dee_hock.htm."

Hofer, C. W., and D. E. Schendel, *Strategy Formulation: Analytical Concepts* (West Publishing Co., St. Paul, MN, 1978).

Kauffman, Jr., D. L., *Systems One: An Introduction to Systems Thinking* (Future Systems, Inc., S. A. Carlton, Publisher, Minneapolis, 1980); originally entitled *The Human Environment: An Introduction to Environmental Systems*, developed under a grant from the Department of Health, Education, and Welfare.

Kauffman, S., *At Home in the Universe: The Search for the Laws of Self-Organization and Complexity* (Oxford University Press, New York and Oxford, 1995).

Ohmae, K., *Borderless World: Power and Strategy in the Intelligent Economy* (HarperCollins, New York, 1991).

Montgomery, R. H., *Auditing Theory and Practice* (Ronald Press, New York, 1912).

Palepu, K. G., V. L. Bernard, and P. M. Healy, *Business Analysis and Valuation Using Financial Statements* (South-Western College Publishing, Cincinnati, 1996).

Porter, M. E., *Competitive Strategy: Techniques for Analyzing Industries and Competitors* (The Free Press, New York, 1980).

Porter, M. E., *Competitive Advantage: Creating and Sustaining Superior Performance* (The Free Press, New York, 1985).

Porter, M. E., *The Competitive Advantage of Nations* (The Free Press, New York, 1990).

Prahalad, C. K., and G. Hamel, "The Core Competence of the Corporation," *Harvard Business Review* 68 (1990), pp. 79 - 91.

Richardson, G. P., *Feedback Thought in Social Science and Systems Theory* (University of Pennsylvania Press, Philadelphia, 1991).

Sanchez, R., A Heene, and H. Thomas, *Dynamics and Competence-Based Competition: Theory and Practice in the New Strategic Management* (Pergamon Press, 1996).

Simms, R., *Levels of Control* (Harvard Business School Press, Boston, 1995).

Stalk, G. Jr., P. Evans, and L. E. Shulman, "Competing on Capabilities: The New Rules of Corporate Strategy" *Harvard Business Review* 17 (1992), pp. 51 - 68.

Van der Heijden, K., *Scenarios: The Art of Strategic Conversation* (John Wiley & Sons Ltd., Chichester, England, 1996).

Watts , R. L. and J. L. Zimmerman, "Agency Problems, Auditing, and the Theory of the Firm: Some Evidence," *Journal of Law and Economics* (1983), pp. 613 - 633.

Wheeler, W., "The Ant Colony as an Organism," *Journal of Morphology* (1911).

Yamey, B. S., "Some Topics in the History of Financial Accounting in England, 1500-1900" reprinted in *Studies in Accounting,* W. T. Baxter and S. Davidson, eds. (The Institute of Chartered Accountants, 1977), pp. 11 - 34.

About the Authors

Timothy B. Bell

Timothy B. Bell is Director, Assurance Services at KPMG Peat Marwick LLP in Montvale, NJ. He earned his Ph.D. in Business Administration from Oklahoma State University in 1981. Dr. Bell has published numerous articles on various accounting and auditing topics in a variety of leading scholarly journals and he is co-editor of the AICPA monograph entitled *Auditing Practice, Research, and Education: A Productive Collaboration* (1995). At KPMG, he has worked on audit process reengineering and development of new assurance services in business ethics and business risk monitoring. Prior to joining KPMG, Dr. Bell was a member of the Accounting Faculty at the University of Texas at Austin.

Frank O. Marrs

Frank O. Marrs, CPA is National Partner in Charge of Assurance Services at KPMG Peat Marwick LLP. Mr. Marrs has extensive auditing experience in several industries, including manufacturing, retail and distribution, financial services, health care and life sciences, and energy. Currently, he manages KPMG's national processes for improving the core audit service, designing and developing new assurance services, and the firm's client satisfaction monitoring process. He has spearheaded the design and rollout of KPMG's Business Measurement Process and heads the team within KPMG that is managing global implementation of the Business Measurement Process.

Ira Solomon

Ira Solomon is the KPMG Peat Marwick Distinguished Professor of Accountancy at the University of Illinois, Urbana-Champaign. He previously has taught at the University of Texas at Austin and at the University of Arizona. His primary research interests are judgment and decision-making in accountancy and auditing and the market for audit services. He has edited several books and has published over thirty articles, which have appeared in a variety of leading scholarly journals. During 1990-91, he was an Audit Research

Fellow in KPMG Peat Marwick's Executive Office and he has served the American Accounting Association Auditing Section as Research Director, Vice-President (Academic), President (1994-95), and Past-President (1995-96). He currently is an Associate Editor of *Accounting Horizons*. Professor Solomon has received several awards for his teaching and publications.

Howard Thomas

Howard Thomas is Dean, College of Commerce and Business Administration, James F. Towey Professor of Strategic Management, and Director of the Office of International Strategic Management all at the University of Illinois at Urbana-Champaign. He holds degrees from Edinburgh University (Ph.D.), University of Chicago (MBA), and London University (MS and BS). He previously held visiting or permanent positions on the faculty of the Australian Graduate School of Management, the London Business School, European Institute of Management (Brussels), the University of Southern California, the University of British Columbia, Massachusetts Institute of Technology, Northwestern University, and INSEAD. He has published numerous books and articles on a wide range of topics, including competitive strategy, risk analysis, managing change, and decision theory and has received several recogitions for outstanding teaching and research. He serves on the Board of Trustees of the Graduate Management Admissions Council and on the Editorial Boards of several major scholarly journals. In 1997, he commences a three-year term as President of the Strategic Management Society.